Native American
Postcolonial
Psychology

SUNY Series in
Transpersonal and Humanistic Psychology

Richard D. Mann, Editor

State University of New York Press

Native American Postcolonial Psychology

Eduardo Duran and Bonnie Duran

Production by Ruth Fisher
Marketing by Fran Keneston

Published by
State University of New York Press, Albany

© 1995   State University of New York

All rights reserved

Printed in the United States of America

No part of this book may be used or reproduced in any manner whatsoever without written permission. No part of this book may be stored in a retrieval system or transmitted in any form or by any means including electronic, electrostatic, magnetic tape, mechanical, photocopying, recording, or otherwise without the prior permission in writing of the publisher.

For information, address State University of New York Press, 90 State Street, Suite 700, Albany, NY 12207

Library of Congress Cataloging-in-Publication Data

Duran, Eduardo, 1949–
    Native American postcolonial psychology / Eduardo Duran and Bonnie Duran.
        p.   cm. — (SUNY series in transpersonal and humanistic psychology)
    Includes bibliographical references (p.   ) and index.
    ISBN 0–7914–2353–0 (cloth : acid-free paper). — ISBN 0–7914–2354–9 (pbk. : acid-free paper)
    1. Indians of North America—
Psychology.   2. Ethnopsychology—
United States.   3. Indian philosophy—United States.   I. Duran, Bonnie, 1955– . II. Series.
    E98.P95D87   1995
    155.8'497—dc20   94–13400
                                                                           CIP

10

This work is respectfully dedicated to
all sundancers and meditators who suffer willingly
for the healing of the earth and its people

By Postcolonial we mean "a social criticism that bears witness to those unequal processes of representation by which the historical experience of the once colonized comes to be framed in the west."

—**Bhabha**

Contents

Foreword	xi
Acknowledgments	xv
Part 1. Theory	1
1. Introduction	3
2. Psychological Worldviews	13
3. The Vehicle	23
4. Theoretical Concerns	55
Part 2. Clinical Praxis	85
5. The Spirit of Alcohol	93
6. Intervention with Families	157
7. The Problem of Suicide	175
8. Community Intervention	185
9. Epilogue	201
Bibliography	209
Index	221

Foreword

It was Autumn 1983 in central California. Made fearless by mild wet winters, the leaves generally refused to turn color. The few exceptions, stirred by genetic memories of four real seasons, were even more powerfully beautiful by contrast. In a very few minutes, yet another beautiful contrast would take place. I was due to supervise a new psychology intern, Eduardo Duran, and it was a part of the week I most looked forward to. Effective supervision sessions are two-way streets for learning. But these sessions were exceptionally productive and full of mystery.

Eduardo, drawing on ethnic tradition (Pueblo and Apache) and psychological framework (Jungian, empowerment, identity and individuation, self-esteem) had found a middle ground for effective clinical intervention. He used dreams, sandtray, cultural and personal metaphor, and nondirective technique in a way simultaneously congruent with millennia of Native American tradition and contemporary psychological practice. More important, this special blend worked. Clients with severe alcohol and substance abuse problems returned to health. Even those with chronic psychosis or character disorder responded. Violent and chaotic home situations improved. My continuing curiosity as a supervisor flourished: How did he do it?

This book is a strong beginning at answering that question. Eduardo Duran began with a fundamental honesty and self-reflection that consistently directed his work. As he encountered new systems and techniques, they were incorporated reliably into a worldview full of hope and history, dream and reality.

In addition to his theoretical perspective, he gives us chapters on specific clinical areas: alcohol and chemical abuse, abused children and families, community intervention by traditional integration. With added case histories, he has designed a practical primer for depth psychotherapy with Native American people, an approach culturally congruent with generations of experience and thought. It is also an excellent model for psychotherapy with other multicultural clients.

Jung is used here as a bridge, not as a foundation. In speaking to psychologists through one of our more familiar frameworks, Dr. Eduardo Duran is being as culturally congruent with clinical practitioners as he has been with his Native American clients. In this way, as he puts it in this book, he can share concepts already old in 1646. Psychology, existing not more than a century, benefits well from this infusion of venerable thought. And action.

His first book, *Archetypal Consultation* (1984), was followed by an appointment as associate professor of psychology at the Pacific Graduate School of Psychology in Palo Alto, California, and Fort Lewis College. Presently he directs the Family and Child Guidance Clinic at the Urban Native American Health Board in Oakland and San Francisco, where I now have the pleasure of learning from Eduardo as friend, colleague, administrator, and adopted uncle. This, his third book is a first-rate guide for practice or classroom. Everyone working in a clinical setting with Native Americans or other people of diverse color and culture should have it on their shelf. And read it.

His tree is of many colors. This is its season.

Postscript

When I wrote the preceding preface to Eduardo Duran's work, Bonnie Guillory-Duran had not yet fully contributed her significant portion, a gift now integrated within the present work.

Perhaps Eduardo's greatest miracle in the midst of one of his most trying times was the discovery of lover and partner Bonnie. To his quiet, understated compassion and power were added new clarity, energy, and compelling vision. Between them now their vision encompasses Eduardo's distant mountains and Bonnie's sparkling cities. Ed's insights now have new and broader applications; Bonnie's catalytic intellect newer implications. They're a great team and wonderful people, but more, the interpersonal focus of Ed Duran's therapy has new energy for prevention and innovation (e.g., urban tribalization). Bonnie is completing a doctoral degree in public health at the University of California at Berkeley and at this writing is assistant professor at UNM medical school.

These two give us hope for the future of our multicultural home in chaotic times. I am reminded that children are art that finish themselves, but fully realized adults are artists that parent the future. Ed and Bonnie's art has opened new doors.

Robert Morgan, Ph.D.
Dean, Professor, Psychologist, Author, and adopted Uncle

Acknowledgments

During the past few years, there have been several events that have led us to reevaluate some of E.D.'s statements in his earlier work *Archetypal Consultation*, also dealing with Native American psychology. In *Archetypal Consultation*, E.D. was constrained by the rules of dissertation writing and had to comply with an institutional lack of understanding for many things that are true and real to us and to other Native American people. This book was undertaken in order to deconstruct some of the subjective assumptions of the Western mind-set. In addition to offering a deconstruction of the Western definition of Native People, this work will continue the ongoing effort to open a dialogue between the Western and traditional ways in which the practices of psychotherapy and healing occur.

We want to give special thanks to our brother Phil Tingley for contributing to the topic of intergenerational posttraumatic stress disorder. Shortly before he went to the spirit world, he came to our apartment in San Francisco and handed us a stack of notes from his back pocket. These notes were the distillation of many talks that we had on the topic over the years. It was important to Phil that these words be put on paper and that these ideas be used in healing the wounds of our people.

E.D. also would like to give thanks to a friend and teacher who helped save him from becoming possessed by Western worldviews as they pertain to not only to psychology, but to life itself. While he was in this plane with us, Clarence was an example of the highest level of compassion that we have known. In his departure from this world he remained impeccably true to his level of awareness, so much so that even death allowed him one last dance. Clarence's teachings will always remain embedded in E.D.'s heart, and his influence is with E.D. as he tries to help people in his day-to-day practice of therapy. Finally, as in previous acknowledgments, we must give due thanks to the spirit of Coyote (as the Sacred Clown), who in his impeccable wisdom continues to carry us into places that are painful, tricky, funny, ridiculous, and unknown. In this process Coyote continues to teach, especially when we least expect to be taught.

There is a long list of people who have contributed to this work. We want to mention a few of the names, although in no way does this encompass all of them nor should anything offensive in this work be considered condoned or attributed to them. We want to thank our parents for going through some extremely difficult times in order to provide for us and help us through the process of becoming educated. Ramon Duran receives a special thanks for never letting us forget who we are and for his incessant prayers. Other people have been helpful by sparking the creative process and/or fostering its unfolding in various environments. A partial list of these people (and other creatures) includes Dan and Rita Freeland, Richard and Arvela Moves Camp, Daryl Standing Elk, Marty, Helen and Murriel Waukazoo, Betty Cooper and family, Kathleen Richard, Anne and Peter Thom, Leslie Gipp, the entire Bratt family, Scarlett Manning, Henry, Ruth, Mark, Pat, and Phill Guillory, Magdelena Avila and family, Susan Cameron, Ed Santos, Nathan Duran, Marlo Friday, Greg Harmon, Rex Harrison, Peggy Barnett, the Brueninger's, Sharon Donnelson, Judy DeJong, Mima Erickson, Helen O'Rourke, Orlando Aranaga, Dianne and John Montoya-Belanger, Arlene Eisen, the Moraga sweat circle, and Drs.

D'Onofrio, Anthony Jaro, Herd, Don Johnson, Minkler, Wallack, Vega, Morgan, Teague, Lukas, May, Room, Gunnel, Ross, Thornton, Giovennetti, Sandner, Weisner, Alaniz, Martinez, Wallerstein, and Beast.

Part 1

Theory

The first part of this book addresses issues of theory as they relate to clinical and community practice. It is critical that the reader have a clear understanding of the issues that have led to the pain felt by many native individuals and communities today. Most of those injuries, we believe, are a direct result of the colonization process.

Colonization has taken place in many other communities across the world during the past five hundred years. There are many similarities in the experience of most colonized people; therefore, much of the discussion in this book is generalizable to other indigenous peoples who have suffered the genocidal effects of colonization. Without a proper understanding of history, those who practice in the disciplines of applied social sciences operate in a vacuum, thereby merely perpetuating this ongoing neocolonialism. It is for this reason that we feel that this theoretical section is an important contribution to social science literature. Not only is this theoretical development useful in understanding the praxis of our model, but the theory is also a step toward legitimizing native epistemological forms.

I

Introduction

And as I looked and wept, I saw that there stood on the north side of the starving camp a Sacred man who was painted red all over his body, and he held a spear as he walked into the center of his people, and there he layed down and rolled. And when he got up it was a fat bison standing there, and where the bison stood a Sacred herb sprang up right where the tree

had been in the center of the nation's hoop. The herb grew and
bore four blossoms on a single stem while I was looking—a blue, a
white, a scarlet and a yellow—and the bright rays of these flashed
to the heavens.

—Black Elk

To Black Elk, this vision symbolized the restoration of the
nations' hoop—the coming together of all the nations in a harmonious manner. Black Elk believed that the nations' hoop
would be restored within seven generations. We are presently in
the time of the restoration of the hoop.

The Problem

The student, practitioner, and academician in the psychological
arena may ask a very valid and practical question: Why another
cross-cultural treatise dealing with Native American psychology?
It seems that psychological literature dealing with some of the
very complex issues of providing theoretical and practical guidance in this area already abounds. As we see it, the existing literature on the subject is sorely lacking in relevance in the form
of theoretical constructions upon which to base a fundamental
approach that actually has some efficacy in ameliorating some of
the problems facing our community.

After a combined three decades of graduate training, clinical practice, and research, the authors have had some ongoing
revelations regarding the use of psychology and the politically
correctly phrased cross-cultural approaches. Early on, we began
to realize that much of the study of cross-cultural issues and the
resultant literature was primarily an exercise that had to be validated by the rules of the academy. It did not take a great reve-
lation to discover that the people who made up the rules of this
academy were predominantly white males. In this sense, knowledge from a cross-cultural perspective must become a caricature
of the culture in order for it to be validated as science or knowledge. Borrowing from the imagery of Frantz Fannon, the study of
colonized peoples must take on a "lactification" or whitening in

order for the produced knowledge to be palatable to the academy. The consequences of such cross-cultural production of knowledge has been ongoing neocolonialism within the discipline of psychology. For example, intelligence testing and sciencing based on eugenics are the root metaphors upon which modern theory and practice are based. From here, we do not need to look far for a critique of psychology—particularly in its cross-cultural formation. Insofar as all the human sciences are founded on the Western philosophical tradition, that tradition itself contains the seeds of psychology's transformation. The "linguistic turn" uncovers our construction based on the binary opposites implicit in Western metaphysics, which in turn constructs all scientific discourse—including psychology. Rather than continuing the "will to power" of control over natural and human processes, new philosophical formulations herald a moral advancement while at the same time negating the teleological progress of history. Feminist studies, cultural studies, and literary criticism are prime examples of the way in which disciplines have been transformed via the incorporation of philosophical insight—much the same way in which Freud reversed the value of the binary opposites of consciousness and unconsciousness. These transformations open the door for different/other models of healing, normalcy, and identity.

The study of cross-cultural thought is a difficult endeavor at best; the outcome of cross-cultural study may be the depreciation of culture rather than its legitimate analysis from another viewpoint. The reality of doing cross-cultural investigation is that most of this analysis is performed through the inoculated gaze of a psychology whose discourse is founded on the premise of the universal subject—the subject of a historical project of emancipation via reason. As long as the language implies that the discourse is cross-cultural, we are perpetuating the notion that other cultures do not have their own valid and legitimate epistemological forms. "Cross-cultural" implies that there is a relative platform from which all observations are to be made, and the platform which remains in place in our neocolonial discipline is that of Western subjectivity. When Western subjectivity is imposed on colonized peoples, not only will the phenomenon under scrutiny evade the lens of positivism, but further hegemony will be imposed on the community in question.

In order for our discipline to lead the way toward a true integration, sincere work must be completed as we move toward a postcolonial paradigm. Quite simply, a postcolonial paradigm would accept knowledge from differing cosmologies as valid in their own right, without their having to adhere to a separate cultural body for legitimacy. Frantz Fannon felt that the third world should not define itself in the terms of European values. Instead, Fannon thought that everything needs to be reformed and thought anew, and that if colonized peoples aren't willing to do this we should leave the destiny of our communities to the Western European mind-set. The year 1992 marked an important anniversary of the onset of colonialism in the New World. In keeping with the spirit of our brother Fannon, thinkers from the third and fourth worlds must create knowledge that is not only new, but is also liberating and healing.

The past five hundred years have been devastating to our communities; the effects of this systematic genocide are currently being felt by our people. The effects of the genocide are quickly personalized and pathologized by our profession via the diagnosing and labeling tools designed for this purpose. If the labeling and diagnosing process is to have any historical truth, it should incorporate a diagnostic category that reflects the effects of genocide. Such a diagnosis would be "acute and/or chronic reaction to colonialism." In this sense, diagnostic policy imposes a structure of normality based in part on the belief in the moral legitimacy and universality of state institutions.

The generation of healing knowledge from the land of the colonist—as has been the history of cross-cultural work—will no longer suffice. Our communities' indigenous forms of knowledge were and continue to be relevant as we face the task of overcoming the colonial mind-set that so many of us have internalized. For this reason, as responsible cross-cultural social scientists, we must address the colonial attitude of our discipline. We cannot continue to reward knowledge that reifies the thought of western Europeans above all others.

We realize that colonization has had an influence on much of the current state of knowledge. In order to have a true integration of thought we must make room for nonlinear thinking, which will yield a true hybrid postcolonial way of expressing subjectivity. As we move into the next millennium, we should not be tolerant of the neocolonialism that runs unchecked through our knowledge-generating systems. We must ensure that the dissemination of thought through journals, media, and other avenues have "gatekeepers" who understand the effects of colonialism and are committed to fighting any perceived act of hegemony on our communities. Postcolonial thinkers should be placed in the positions that act as gatekeepers of knowledge in order to insure that western European thought be kept in its appropriate place.

If psychology continues on its present course, the judgment of history will continue to be unkind—as already described by Michel Foucault in *Madness and Civilization* (1967). It is no longer acceptable for psychology to continue to be the enforcement branch of the secularized Judeo-Christian myth. Through the worshipping of logical positivism, our discipline has been a coconspirator in the devastation and control of those peoples who are not subsumed under a white, male, heterosexual, Christian subjectivity.

The Newtonian and Cartesian fundamentalists who continue to entrench themselves in kneeling at the altar of science must analyze and deconstruct their actions anew. A very simplistic analysis will illustrate that their so-called objectification of science is nothing but ongoing social control and hegemony. Our discipline prefers to think that psychological thought exists in an acontextual form, emerging as the immaculate conception of the past century. In reality, psychological thought as an offshoot of medicine has been gestating since the Middle Ages and continues to be implicated in an ongoing system of social control as it was during the heyday of the papacy. These notions are sure to disrupt the linear thinking of most of our objective scientific brothers and sisters in the profession. A postcolonial diagnosis for such objective scientists would perhaps be, "chronic and/or acute Cartesian anxiety disorder." Fortunately, this is a disorder that has a good prognosis when treated with some of the new postcolonial therapeutic interventions. Postcolonial psychology will not operate on the basis of a logic of equivalence—A:non-A—but rather on a logic of difference—A:B. Postcolonial psychology will celebrate all diverse ways of life rather than comparing others to what they are not.

The current literature illustrates how contemporary service delivery is still failing not only Native Americans but other ethnic groups as well. Stanley Sue has found that "regardless of utilization rates, all of the ethnic-minority groups had significantly higher dropout rates than whites" (1987, p. 37). One of the most important factors in the failure of the mental health delivery system is an inability of therapists to provide relevant forms of treatment to ethnic populations.

Most of the attempts at providing services to Native American people have ended in failure. For the most part, the blame for this failure has been placed on the patient instead of on a delivery system that is still brazen with overtones of the 1800s Department of War policy: assimilation and/or termination of Native American people. Most providers are trained only in delivering services to the majority/dominant population. Usually, therapists are completely unaware of the life experiences of the ethnic minority patient. In earlier works—*Archetypal Consultation* (1984) and *Transforming the Soul Wound* (1990)—a theoretical construct was initiated (though never fully developed). This construct was the result of the integration of Jungian psychology and community consultation concepts. The resulting mental health model was implemented in a Native American community in central and northern California and, when measured by some standard evaluation methods, was assessed as having some success.

Since the initial success of this program, there have been further developments in the way psychology has been delivered to the aforementioned group of people. The program has expanded into a prevention and treatment model that has yielded a successful history of Native American people seeking relevant treatment for some of the problems they encounter as part of living in a colonialistic setting. The purpose here is not to suggest that these paradigms are the final answer to the mental health problems in Native American country. Instead, we would like to point out some possible weaknesses that may be inherent in the models that were developed and offer some new solutions that have emerged after decades of clinical practice and research with Native American people.

In the past few years, much literature has emerged dealing with the issue of cross-cultural approaches. Although as yet no one has proposed a model that actually has had a significant level of success, some articles on Native American psychology have been written. Most of the literature having to do with Native Americans continues to focus on the lack of relevant approaches to psychological treatment as well as to paint a very grim picture of the extent of the problems afflicting the native American community. Most approaches implemented on Native peoples are ongoing attempts at further colonization of their lifeworld. Alcoholism, chemical dependency, and high rates of suicide continue to plague these communities. Programs that have the responsibility for addressing these problems appear impotent in the face of such a herculean task, although there are some isolated instances of success in treatment.

There continues to be discussion about integrating Western and traditional approaches in order to offer a solution to the problem; for the most part, however, the effort has remained in the realm of academic discussion. The problem is not so much with traditional practitioners in the Native American community as with the Western practitioners. Western practitioners approach traditional healing methods with skepticism while expecting absolute faith from the traditionals in orthodox Western-oriented therapeutic strategies. A bridge between these two camps must be built. The bridging task is more difficult than it might appear, since most Western practitioners are deeply entrenched in a worldview that will not allow for openness outside of rational empirical thought processes. In spite of the problems of bridging the worlds there are many non-Native American people who are embracing traditional concepts and actually portraying themselves as traditional medicine people or shamans. When Westerners portray themselves in this manner, they only increase the existing gap, since the Native American community perceives these impostors as exploitative and disrespectful.

Purpose and Approach

The purpose of this book is to shed some light on how to approach these differing worldviews and the lack of understanding that exists between them; in so doing, we may begin to integrate these worldviews. By elaborating on models previously espoused in *Archetypal Consultation* and *Transforming the Soul Wound*, we offer some new ideas as to how issues of psyche can best be understood using the analytic methods of Archetypal psychology combined with Native American cosmology.

In this book, the problems of living a healthy and balanced life in the Native American community are honestly dealt with from the perspective of the community. The term *soul wound* is delineated and placed into the perspective of practical clinical intervention. The uses of Jungian typology are explored as they provide a construct that catapults this treatise into a new perspective. The authors demonstrate how the knowledge that has existed in the native community for hundreds of years directly addresses many problems faced by the community today. In so doing we feel that we are offering a long overdue legitimization of epistemological forms.

In the Clinical Praxis part of the book, the first area of discussion is alcoholism. We offer a review of the literature in this area, as well as some views of alcoholism from the perspective of oral tradition. The literature review is presented in academic fashion as is customary, and the traditional component is offered in a manner that reflects Traditional discussion. We then follow the alcohol section with some case examples illustrating the actual provision of treatment.

A brief discussion on working with Native American families is then offered. The sandtray is discussed as it is used in the assessment and treatment of children and families. The family discussion is followed by a chapter on suicide and, finally, by a chapter on community approaches to delivering services to Native American people.

In this book, we also include some discussion of how some of this work has been implemented in the treatment of a range of psychological diagnostic categories. We offer strategies that have emerged during the process of working therapeutically with individual clients and with communities. Some of these strategies have emerged from the despair of not having anything to offer to the client who is suffering greatly. The strategies that have emerged in this work are seen within the context of transforming a trauma that has been a painful part of the Native American community for many decades. As part of the honest "seeing" of things, we also discuss some of the parallels between shamanism and psychotherapy.

The epilogue of the book reflects on some sociopolitical issues that are inherent in working with Native American people. The fact that the Native American community has such a great number of problems is addressed from a sociohistorical perspective.

This book describes some of the notions needed in order to understand the worldview of Native American people. The purpose is not to encapsulate the experience of being a Native American so as to give the reader a blueprint of this perspective. Instead, the intent is to give the reader the necessary tools required to understand the theoretical discussion as well as the specific treatment strategies in this book. It is our hope that this discussion will be useful to therapists, counselors, paraprofessionals, academics, students, and community activists, advocates, and consultants.

2

Psychological Worldviews

The Third World ought not to be content to define itself in the terms of values which have preceded it. . . . everything needs to be reformed and everything thought out anew. . . . If we want to turn Africa into a new Europe, and America into a new Europe, then let us leave the destiny of our countries to

Europeans. They will know how to do it better than the most gifted among us.

—Frantz Fannon

Toward Understanding the Native American Worldview

Attempting to describe enough of the Native American worldview (also called "cosmology" in this book) so that the rest of this discussion makes sense is a difficult task. The description that we offer in this section is useful for operationally defining some of the terms and ideas in this book, but it is not an actual definition of what the experience of the Native American worldview is. In order to present a discussion of the experience of being in the world as a Native American, we would have to devote an entire thesis to the topic (since there is so much cultural diversity among different tribes), which would exceed the scope of this discussion.

One of the first ideas to be kept in mind when thinking about the Native American worldview from a Western perspective is that the native temporal approach to the world is different from that of Western people. Western thought conceptualizes history in a linear temporal sequence, whereas most Native American thinking conceptualizes history in a spatial fashion. Temporal thinking means that time is thought of as having a beginning and end; spatial thinking views events as a function of space or where the event actually took place. Understanding the space-time difference in conceptualizing history is necessary in order for the therapist to realize that the two ways of thinking are different yet are part of the same continuum. Although the therapist/social scientist may be interested in *when* something happened, the client/community may be more interested in *where* the event took place. The idea of being in space versus time does not have to be a rigid one, and the client may or may not want to relate events in a more space-time integrated approach, although time may not have the same linear quality that it does for the Western person.[1]

The Native American worldview is a systemic approach to being in the world that can best be categorized as process thinking, as opposed to the content thinking found in the Western worldview. Process thinking is best described as a more action and "eventing" approach to life versus a world of object relationships. Some indigenous languages, for instance, are languages in which phenomena are experienced as the process of events. Western Indo-European languages describe the world predominantly by means of nouns or as relationships between objects, not as events.

Another crucial worldview difference of which the Western therapist must be cognizant is that of noncompartmentalization of experience. In Western experience it is common to separate the mind from the body and spirit and the spirit from mind and body. Within the Native American worldview this is a foreign idea. Most Native American people experience their being in the world as a totality of personality and not as separate systems within the person. This becomes more complex for the Western therapist/social scientist when the idea of the personality being part of all creation is discussed. Thus the Native American worldview is one in which the individual is a part of all creation, living life as one system and not in separate units that are objectively relating with each other. The idea of the world or creation existing for the purpose of human domination and exploitation— the core of most Western ideology—is a notion that is absent in Native American thinking.

Any psychology of Native American people must have a direct impact on the way that any type of relationship is experienced. The experience of therapy or healing is no exception to the experience of being in the world. The need for healing can be explained by the fact that the client/community has lost the ability to be in harmony with the life process of which the client/ community is a part.

Life experiences are process, which makes "being" a different experience than that in which the world can be explained by discussion of content. Whereas the Western approach to the

---

1. For a deeper discussion of worldview, the reader is referred to Vine Deloria's book *God is Red* (1992).

world is one in which everything is categorized and named, the Native American way of being in the world involves a relationship and moving in harmony with the seasons, the wind, and all of creation.

The practice of Western psychotherapy entails a linear passage of time in which the client/community can resolve or be cured from its present problems. In Native American thinking the idea of time having to pass in order to receive healing or blessing makes no sense. In Native American healing the factor that is of importance is intensity versus passage of time. For instance, if the person dances with great intensity, that person achieves as much as the person who dances for a long time (if time is the only variable). When the Western therapist treats a Native American person, time passing may not be as crucial as the intensity of the therapeutic process.[2]

The process of psychotherapy is an arena in which the integration of worldviews is very important because psychotherapy attempts to restore balance in human beings. The restoration of balance demands that a relationship between psyche and matter (world, creation) be one of harmony; this is one of the paradigms that Jung discussed in his attempt to bridge the gap of psyche and matter that existed in his world. For Carl Jung the bridge was crossed through the use of symbols, and he believed that symbols provided the transcendent function that balances psyche and matter.

When working with traditional peoples, the therapeutic method must take into account the way in which traditional healers think. The notion of a personal layer of psyche surrounded by a tribal or ethnic strata lends itself to useful explanations in the arena of psychological work. Jung theorized that

---

2. We want to impress upon the reader that this discussion is a generalization, since there are tribes that do not think in this manner. The intertribal glossing in which we are engaged is necessary in order to stay within the scope of the project at hand. In no way do we pretend to understand and speak for all Indians—this would be an act of colonization. In postcolonial paradigms, we feel that by discussing this limitation some honesty is incorporated. This honesty is a small step toward respect.

a symbol functions as the entity that transforms energy in the psyche. Culture plays an important role in the transformation of energy by providing a symbolic system that steers and guides the transformation of psychic energy for that particular culture. The development of the psyche cannot be accomplished by intention alone and according to Jung, "it needs the attraction of the symbol, whose value quantum exceeds that of the cause. . . . If man lived altogether instinctively and automatically, the transformation could come about in accordance with purely biological laws" (1960, p. 25) Since people do not live instinctively, we cannot simply resort to biological laws and explanations and must continue to work with laws that apply to the psyche in a purely psychological fashion.

Specific Problems with Western Psychological Worldviews

Western psychology (most psychology studied and taught is Western) has undergone a natural evolutionary process that has roots so deeply entrenched in classic Western philosophy that many scholars agree it is simply a footnote to Plato. In psychology, it matters little if the model or theory is Freudian, Jungian, or any other of the classical or contemporary theories. The critical factor in cross-cultural psychology is a fundamentally different way of being in the world. In no way does Western thinking address any system of cognition except its own. Given that Judeo-Christian belief systems include notions of the Creator putting humans in charge of all creations, it is easy to understand why this group of people assumes that it also possesses the ultimate way of describing psychological phenomena for all of humanity. In reality, the thought that what is right comes from one worldview produces a narcissistic worldview that desecrates and destroys much of what is known as culture and cosmological perspective.

The notion of the white man as a destructive entity unleashed on our world has been illustrated by Jung:

As soon as I was outside our white civilization, I saw what Europeans are like. We look awful. The Chinese call us devils and it is true, thin cruel lips, and our wrinkles are uncanny. And we are always intent on something no devil can understand. . . . From Europe, that half-island, the white man came in ships, bringing awful diseases and fire-water, and even intentionally selling infected clothing to destroy the population, as they did in the South Seas. Wherever the white man went, there was hell for the other nations; one has to be outside to understand. The white man is a very beast devouring the Earth, the whole world trembles at him. Such Christianity is a compensation, a hellish lie. (1984, p. 337)

It appears as if Jung had come to grips with the essence of what the Western psyche is in quest of, and it is this very individualistic ideology that is at the root of most clinical and research psychology practiced in the world today. It is little wonder that Native American people prefer to remain alienated from Western therapies and choose not to work on their psychological problems rather than to be further exploited by a therapeutic system that has its root metaphors deeply entrenched in the causes of the presenting problems themselves.

The problem of irrelevant research and clinical practice would not be so destructive to Native American people if institutional racism did not pervade most of the academic settings for research and theoretical construction. These institutions not only discredit thinking that is not Western, but also engage in practices that imply that people who do not prescribe to their worldview are genetically inferior. Stephen Jay Gould refers to the practice of valuing cultural experiences which are Western and white over any other cultural experience as biological determinism (1981, p. 325).

A good example of how some of the ideology of biological determinism affects people is seen in the field of psychometric assessment. The relevant literature is filled with studies showing cultural bias and outright racist practices, yet researchers continue to use the same racist tools to evaluate the psyche of Native American peoples. The very essence of Western science as applied to psychology is permeated with biological determinism that has as its sole purpose the demonstration of white superiority. Many examples can be cited of Native American people losing their freedom, being sterilized, or losing their children simply because they were not able to pass the white standards of a psychometric test.

Even though there are many obstacles to the development of relevant and practical psychotherapeutic interventions for Native American people, the fact that there are difficulties does not mean that we should simply despair and give up hope. We must keep an open mind by following the advice of Sitting Bull: "Take what is good from the White Man and let's make a better life for our children." There are valuable ideas in the Western world; the authors believe that by integrating worldviews and psychological understanding, we can develop a model that will benefit Native American people as well as others. By reinterpreting some of the theoretical constructs developed by Jung, and by taking this reinterpreted psychology and integrating it with traditional psychology and other native epistemologies, we can arrive at ideas with some theoretical and clinical relevance.

Problems in Implementing Traditional Approaches

Traditional approaches or practices are based on the concepts of illness and healing held by the group and may provide some insights into orthodox strategies as they are implemented among the Native American community. Traditional approaches are still used, but these approaches are not very common in certain groups because of a loss of skills due to the conquest of Native American peoples. These traditional interventions receive criticism from the orthodox camp, and orthodox Western (usually medical) approaches do not accept or are not aware of indigenous practices.

A very general and useful analysis of traditional concepts of illness and healing was formulated by F. E. Clements in 1932, and those notions are still useful in understanding traditional concepts when seen from a Western platform. Clements has provided some guidelines that are still helpful in understanding non-Western concepts of illness and healing.

The most widely held belief about illness is the personal belief that a diseased object has intruded the body, thus causing sickness. The obvious therapy for this type of illness is having the object removed by physical means such as cutting or bleeding and sucking out the diseased objects or body parts. The Westerner does not have to stretch his imagination any further than the surgical table upon which all of this removal and sucking of bad blood and diseased organs is performed daily in all hospitals across the United States. There is so much belief in object extraction in our society that surgery is used almost as a placebo, creating the belief that the physician is actually performing the needed cure.

According to Clements, the second most popular belief about illness involves the loss of soul. The illness in this case may derive from two means. One cause of the illness is the departure of the soul from the body. The second possible cause of this illness is the theft or abduction of the soul by ghosts or sorcerers. The treatment for this illness comes through the restoration of the soul by the healer. Of the traditional concepts, soul loss may be the most difficult for the Western worldview to accept. However, there is common ground between the two different paradigms. Many therapists talk about patients being beside themselves, loss of ego, and alienation; the task, then, is to place the person back in touch with reality.

Another belief about illness involves spirit intrusion and/or possession, which occurs when the person is made ill by an evil spirit invading the body and causing the illness. In this case. the therapy may be done by three different means: the spirit may be expelled mechanically by bleeding, beating, or by presenting noises and smells; by transferring the spirit to another being; or by exorcism.

A concept of illness that may have more cross-cultural applications is the illness being caused by a transgression against social or religious mores. According to some anthropological accounts, serious sickness and even death may be possible due to the breach of taboo. The most common treatment for this condition is confession or catharsis to a healer or priest. This notion is closely related to the practice of psychotherapy in which many of the sessions are used by the patient to clear him/herself of the guilt of the actual or perceived violations of some societal taboo or norm.

Sorcery is a method whereby sickness is caused by an individual who has power and can will an illness on another individual. The most common treatment for this form of illness is an appeal to a person who has the power to counter the spell, thus alleviating the sickness. There are some parallels in psychotherapy where a therapist either consciously or unconsciously inflicts pathology on the patient. In this case, the usual cure is to go to another therapist who can counter the illness, thus countering the evil therapist's actions.

Because of the tremendous influx of Native American people into urban areas, providing traditional therapy is further complicated. By leaving traditional lands and moving to where there are more economic opportunities, it becomes difficult to maintain traditional ways. Yet the bleak realities of staying in a place where there is little hope of finding work places the modern Native American in a double bind. In the San Francisco Bay Area there are presently 100,000 Native American people from at least three hundred different tribal groups. The idea of being able to serve all of these people in a relevant manner becomes extremely difficult, and one must begin to find commonalities not only within different traditional groups, but within the orthodox Western camp as well.

The lack of traditional medicine people in the urban setting presents a major difficulty in the attempt to serve the Native American community. In order for a client to be treated by a traditional healer, s/he must undergo substantial expense due to the distances that must be traveled in order to be treated traditionally. As the reader may suspect, the practitioner who is dealing with severe problems in this setting must be creative and flexible if s/he is to be of any use to the individual or community.

3

The Vehicle

There is always a dream dreaming us.

—Kalahari Bushmen

Social Science / Historical Perspective

Most literature on the health problems of Native American people demonstrates that the genesis of the problems are

23

found in the area of psychological dysfunction. Health status statistics are grim, and it seems as if many problems have a very high incidence in the Native American community. Alcoholism rates have reached enormous proportions, anxiety and depression are high, suicide rates are the highest for any ethnic group, and school dropouts are rated as high as 70 percent in some communities.

Why should Native Americans be so plagued with problems of this nature? This question arose regularly during E.D.'s work with native people in central California. In order to gain some insight into this issue, E.D. simply posed the question to the community. Most people responded with issues of injustice, the conquest, the dishonored treaties, and so on. In this, a common thread was found that weaves across much of the pain and suffering found in the Native American community across the United States and perhaps the entire Western Hemisphere. The image which became most binding and meaningful to the authors and to some of the other people working in other Native American communities is the concept termed the *soul wound.*

If one accepts the *terms soul, psyche, myth, dream,* and *culture* as part of the same continuum that makes people's experience of being in the world their particular reality, then one can begin to understand the soul wound. The notion of soul wound is one which is at the core of much of the suffering that indigenous peoples have undergone for several centuries. This notion needs to be understood in a historical context in order to be useful to the modern therapist providing therapeutic services and consultation to the Native American community.

Historically, Native Americans have been one of the most neglected groups of people in this country in education, health, and mental health. The insignificant amount of ethical research and program funding in mental health in a population that clearly has been in dire need is indicative of the level of this neglect (Duran 1989). Native activism resulting in the 1975 Native American Self-Determination and Educational Assistance Act has ushered in a new era of native scholarship and tribal control on research and in program planning. This newly legitimized push for self-determination, unfortunately, does not immediately rectify problems rooted in years of white-biased research and social engineering.

One important barrier encountered while attempting to conduct research in the Native American community is the residual feelings still fresh in most Native American memories for the colonizing techniques of the anthropologists and other well-meaning albeit arrogant social scientists. A high level of distrust exists among Native American people to anyone asking questions, regardless of the good promised by the results of the research and often regardless of the tribal affiliations of the researcher. This suspicion and lack of trust on the part of tribal leaders may be detrimental to research interests but are not necessarily damaging to tribal interests.

The empirical methodological paradigm of most research contributes to the lack of its acceptability within Native American nations and communities. Even when academicians pretend to study cultures different from their own, most dare not ask the most logical of all questions: What is the point of reference for the interpretation of data? Sinha eloquently captures this problem: "There are several reasons for this retardation. First, modern psychology has been a product of the West and has been imported almost wholesale to Third World countries. . . . Too often, problems taken up for research have been mere replications of whatever had been done in Europe or the United States with little relations to the needs of the country. Such unimaginative replications of Western research have been decried and called caricatures of Westerns studies" (1984, p. 20).

To assume that phenomena from another worldview can be adequately explained from a totally foreign worldview is the essence of psychological and philosophical imperialism. This lack of theoretical and clinical relevance is clearly demonstrated all over the third and fourth worlds and is presently the topic of theoretical debate within the academy. Postcolonial practitioners and intellectuals have convincingly discredited the Eurocentric histographic narrative of people of color (Murray 1991; Said 1978), and have delineated how this production of meaning not only fails to capture any "truth" of native and tribal lives but also infiltrates native lifeworlds in the form of "epistemic violence" (Spivak 1990, p. 126). Social scientists have been rewriting tribal canonical texts (i.e., ritual) via anthropology and other disciplines since first contact and therein have produced meaning that has changed and distorted tribal understandings or forced them underground. Clinical psychology as well as research-oriented psychology is extremely narrow-minded. These fields' assumptions are based on a utilitarian worldview. According to Sinha "its orientation is basically micro-social, concentrating itself almost entirely on personal characteristics of the individual actors in social processes rather than on sociostructural factors" (1984, p. 21). Western empirical research is based on the illusion of objectivity with a transhistorical, transcultural orientation. It operates within an a priori, essentialist Cartesian model of a unified, rational, autonomous subject, the construction of which is problematized in the work of French poststructuralism and German critical theory. Guha and Spivak, Derridian deconstructionists, posit a decentered self: "that which operates as a subject may be part of an immense discontinuous network of strands that may be termed politics, ideology, economics, history, sexuality, language and so on" (1988, p. 12). Social scientific investigation into domestic violence deproblematizes the material history of science as well. Foucault (1973) brilliantly dissected what he called "technologies of power" authorized by the sciences of medicine. He illustrated that, far from objective statements of truth, the science of medicine emerged fully implicated in practices of domination. The objectification of Native American family violence deprives it of its material history and hence of a crucial aspect of its truth. Context plays no part when the goal is transcendental truths about human nature. Sinha believes, however, that within this orientation "one is disappointed by their artificiality, triviality, and lack of relevance to real-life psychological phenomena. The methodology of psychological research has to be broadened to make it more relevant for the study of complex social problems facing Third World countries in the process of development" (1984, p. 21). Some postmodern theorists have gone so far as to say "once we give up metaphysical attempts to find a 'true self' for man (sic), we can only appear as the contingent historical selves we find ourselves to be" (Rorty 1992, p. 62). The history of native/white relations since colonization not only presents the context of the treatment of family violence but must also illuminate the knowledge/power construction of the native subject that has infiltrated native subjectivity and identity.

Successful clinical interventions are not possible in a Native American setting unless the provider or agency is cognizant of the sociohistorical factors that have had a devastating effect on the dynamics of the Native American family. Beginning in the late 1800s, the U.S. government implemented policies whose effect was the systematic destruction of the Native American family system under the guise of educating Native Americans in order to assimilate them as painlessly as possible into Western society, while at the same time inflicting a wound to the soul of Native American people that is felt in agonizing proportions to this day. This pain is quite obvious when the family system is examined in a clinical context that employs honesty as a fundamental premise of prevention/intervention.

Skepticism concerning the applicability of a purely psychological model to represent family violence problems for Native American peoples does not mean denying the need or contribution of psychology in the prevention or treatment of behavior problems. Rather, our purpose is to look deeper into the multidimensional nature of mental health for fresh perspectives and empowering interventions instead of privileging a universalistic scientific discourse over the voice of the subjects. A richer perspective is vital in the work of mental health professionals who presently are involved in reeducation and resocialization into appropriate family behaviors, the definitions of which are politically discursive.

The clinical perspectives outlined in this book are not intended to essentialize native people into some stereotypical identity, but rather to create counterhegemonic discourse and to uncover deep-rooted pain that makes many clinicians from European-American backgrounds uncomfortable.

Internalized Oppression

The destruction of Native American families was, in part, carried out through the coerced attendance of Native American children at boarding schools designed to forcefully remove Native American culture. The child had to live away from the parents for the duration of the school year and was not allowed to speak the native language or engage in any activities that were remotely connected to the child's culture. The child was often forced to practice Christianity and was taught that any religious belief that s/he had from his/her own tribal belief system was of the devil and was to be supplanted by the Judeo-Christian belief system. During the acculturation era there were a few white Christians who questioned this practice, but for the most part the boarding schools were effective in their effort in destroying traditional Native American culture.

Once the idea of family is eradicated from the thinking and lifeworld of an individual, cultural reproduction cannot occur. The problems that we face today in the process of intervening with Native American families are problems caused by a conspiracy that was implemented over one hundred years ago. Since the governmental policy was so effective, many times the task in working with families involves education as to what the concept of family actually is. A therapist that approaches a family session in a way which does not account for the history of ethnocide perpetrated against Native Americans is him/herself a coconspirator with that history as s/he proceeds with "blaming the victim."

Native American people have been subjected to one of the most systematic attempts at genocide in the world's history. At the beginning of the colonization process in North America there were over 10 million Native American people living on the continent. By the year 1900 there were only 250,000 people left (Thornton 1986). For over five hundred years Europeans have attempted to subjugate, exterminate, assimilate, and oppress Native American people. The effects of this subjugation and extermination have been devastating both physically and psychologically. Whole tribal groups have been completely exterminated; most of the land that was inhabited by Native Americans has been stolen. The policies of the U.S. government toward Native American people are shameful, particularly as they have been enacted by a government that preaches freedom and democracy. Even more shameful is the fact that this government maintained a policy of termination of Native American people until recently.

Once a group of people have been assaulted in a genocidal fashion, there are psychological ramifications. With the victim's complete loss of power comes despair, and the psyche reacts by internalizing what appears to be genuine power—the power of the oppressor. The internalizing process begins when Native American people internalize the oppressor, which is merely a caricature of the power actually taken from Native American people. At this point, the self-worth of the individual and/or group has sunk to a level of despair tantamount to self-hatred. This self-hatred can be either internalized or externalized.

Research has demonstrated the grim reality of internalized hatred resulting in suicide (Duran 1989). Native American people have been dying in great numbers due to suicide. Another way in which the internalized self-hatred is manifested symptomatically is through the deaths of massive numbers by alcoholism.

When self-hatred is externalized, we encounter a level of violence within the community that is unparalleled in any other group in the country. Native Americans have the highest rate of violent crimes of any group, with homicide and suicide rates that are almost double the U.S. all-races rates (Abbas 1982; French and Hornbuckle 1982). What is remarkable about this violence is that for the most part, it is directed at other Native Americans. When we interpret relations in a Native American context as all Native Americans being immediate family, then our community has the highest rate of domestic violence of any group. If domestic violence is defined as violence within the Native American nuclear family, no incidence studies are currently available to us. However, from decades of work in the Native American community, the authors can attest to the astronomical incidence of domestic violence within the Native American nuclear family.

Much of the domestic violence in the Native American community can be interpreted as a venting of anger toward someone that is helpless and as a reminding of the perpetrator of himself. The root of the anger is toward the oppressor, but any attempts at catharting anger toward its root result in swift retaliation by the oppressor. This is obvious in the high rates of Native Americans in prisons (one out of every three Native American males will be imprisoned during their lifetime). Therefore, it is safer for the perpetrator to cathart his/her anger on a helpless family member who represents the hated part of him/ herself.

This aggression serves a dual purpose. The perpetrator of violence can achieve momentary catharsis and relief while at the same time destroying the part of him/herself that reminds him/ her of that helplessness and lack of hope. In essence, the individual attacks his or her own projection in a person close by. Meanwhile, the person inflicting the violence may or may not be aware that he/she really would like to vent this rage on the oppressor.

Intergenerational Posttraumatic Stress Disorder

The problem with the perpetrator of domestic violence is that the oppressor becomes such an integral part of his/her personality that s/he cannot differentiate that part of the personality from his/her real personality. This integration of the oppressor by the personality does not occur overnight; it has been systematically interwoven into the fabric of the Native American family for generations. Most of the literature on intergenerational transmission of posttraumatic stress disorder (PTSD) has emerged from research done with victims of the Nazi Holocaust. Many of the dynamics in effect in the Jewish experience are similar to those of the Native American experience, with the crucial exception that the world has not acknowledged the Holocaust of native people in this hemisphere. This lack of acknowledgment remains one of the stumbling blocks to the healing process of Native American people. The inherent denial keeps the colonial perpetrators trapped in an aura of secrecy and continuing alienation, since their acts continue to haunt them with guilt and existential emptiness.

In a study by T. Shoshan it was found that "violent sudden separation from their closest family members determined the extent of survivors' individual traumas. Uncompleted mourning and the depression and somber states of mind it created were absorbed by their children from birth on. Children of survivors react to the lack of memories and absence of dead family members" (1989, p. 193). A few generations before the effects of the Jewish Holocaust, Native American people were suddenly separated not only from loved family members but also from the Earth, another close relative.

Z. Solomon, M. Kotter, and M. Mikulincer, in a study conducted on children of Holocaust survivors (1988), found that PTSD was generationally cumulative. Children of Holocaust survivors who were themselves involved in war experienced more PTSD than those involved in war whose parents were not Holocaust survivors. Krell reports that "in my nearly twenty years of psychiatric practice, there has been a steady stream of Holocaust survivors and their children presenting with various problems. In the last decade a number of 'child survivors' have also presented with first breakdowns, depressive or otherwise, and always with strong links to the Holocaust experience" (1990, p. 18). It is not difficult to make the case that similar psychology is in operation with Native American people and their descendants who were subjected to a Holocaust experience.

Many of the Native American people who survived the onslaught were not only physically abused but also psychologically tormented. The level of abuse could have easily provided a workshop on technique even for the most sophisticated diabolical minds in Hitler's regime. Moskovitz and Krell, referring to the Jewish Holocaust found that "inevitably, these children, now adults, have lived their lives with a series of perplexing questions and fragmented memories. The normal developmental tasks of growing up were mutilated beyond recognition by the traumas of loss and grief, danger and fear, hatred and chaos" (1990, p. 81). If these traumas are not resolved in the lifetime of the person suffering such upheaval, it is unthinkable that the person will not fall into some type of dysfunctional behavior that will then become the learning environment for their children. Once these children grow up with fear, rage, danger, and grief as the norm, it is little wonder that family problems of all types begin to emerge within the family system.

Another form of ongoing trauma is through the forced acculturation of Native American people. Native American people are constantly under extreme pressure to assimilate the lifeworld of the perpetrators of the Holocaust. Acculturation stress is a continuing factor in the perpetration of anxiety, depression, and other symptomatology that is associated with PTSD:

> The concept of acculturative stress refers to one kind of stress, that in which the stressors are identified as having their source in the process of acculturation, often resulting in a particular set of stress behaviors that include anxiety, depression, feelings of marginality and alienation, heightened psychosomatic symptoms and identity confusion. Acculturative stress is thus a phenomenon that may underlie a reduction in the health status of individuals, including physical, psychological and social health. (Williams and Berry 1991, p. 634)

Through years of working in health and social service settings with subsequent generations of Native American people, the authors have developed a scheme of the progression of PTSD. The following stages are offered in order to facilitate our understanding of intergenerational posttraumatic stress disorder in the Native American community:

First Contact. During the initial contact between native and colonial cultures, there occurred an environmental shock. The lifeworld as had been known for centuries became threatened, and in most cases that lifeworld was systematically destroyed. The makeup of the lifeworld consisted of all cultural experience, with spirituality at its core. The psychological trauma perpetrated by such an intrusion had collective impact at the beginning of what was to become a process of ongoing loss and separation. This loss and separation was not only from loved ones, but was also a loss of the relationship the people had with their daily world. These losses were not allowed the time for proper bereavement and grief process, thus adding to the wound in the Native American collective psyche.

Economic Competition. During this phase of the trauma, Native American people were exposed to similar dynamics as in the first contact stage. Lands, wildlife, and so on that were used for sustenance were destroyed or taken by the European settlers. The European attitude toward the environment was diametrically opposed to the attitude prevailing in most Native American communities. Whereas the Native American psychology was one of oneness and harmony with the environment, the European attitude was one of taking without regard to the cyclical nature of relating to the world. Western Europeans approached the environment in a utilitarian manner conducive to consumption of the world rather than living with it. This utilitarian psychology was and is foreign and in opposition to the cosmology of Native American people.

Invasion War Period. This phase of the contact was brutal and genocidal in the proportions of its implementation. The United States government implemented a policy of extermination of Native American people through the use of military force. Needless to say, this type of policy greatly impacted the psyche of Native American people since many were killed or removed from traditional homelands by force. Many Native American people acquired a refugee syndrome as they were displaced from their loved ones and from the land.

Subjugation and Reservation Period. As part of the military campaigns the Native American nations were not only subdued by force, but also were relocated. Part of the U.S. scenario included the forced relocation of Native Americans to areas unfamiliar to them. The unfamiliarity of the reservations added to the subjugation by destroying the culture, which was based on the traditional land base that the Native American nations had up to that time.

Boarding School Period. One of the most devastating policies implemented by the government were boarding schools, which were primarily designed to destroy the fabric of Native American life—the family unit. Once the family unit was destroyed the culture was sure to suffer and the plan of termination of Native American nations would then be complete. Native American children were forcefully removed from their families and taken to a distant place where they were assimilated into the white worldview. These children were not permitted to speak their native language or to have any type of relationship with their tribal roots. Children were physically made to look as close to their white counterparts as possible in order to strip them of their Native American-ness. Boys were given short haircuts, and colonial clothes of the day were to be worn (even though at times they did not fit); the boys were placed in classes training for a trade, and the girls were usually taught how to sew and perform other housework.

Forced Relocation and Termination Period. One of the final surges of the federal government's termination of Native American people took place in the 1950s. When Native American people were forcibly relocated from reservations into large metropolitan areas such as San Francisco and Los Angeles. Families were promised housing, jobs, and other support in order to make the transition. The reality of the relocation was that these families were dumped into the cities with no support, making their survival very difficult. Many families did not survive; the ones that did continue to experience the effects of the forced relocation as manifested by the refugee syndrome as well as the concentration camp syndrome.

The abuse that Native American people faced and continue to face from the assault waged by the U.S. government was felt at all levels. This abuse included physical, emotional, spiritual, and sexual abuse. The dynamics of such abuse on an individual are well known to clinical practitioners: the victim has the tendency of internalizing the abuse and becoming like the abuser him/herself. The decades of abuse of Native Americans in turn formulated what can best be described as hybrid family systems in which the traditional family system no longer existed. This trauma broke the systems apart, and a new negative and dysfunctional ideology was incorporated into the Native American family system. This dysfunction and oppression have been internalized to such a degree that the oppressed members of the family seemingly want to continue to be oppressed or abused. "the oppressed all too often desire their oppression, either because they code their desire within machines of domination, or because the machines of domination produce their desire" (Bogue 1990, p. 106).

After so many decades of abuse and internalizing of pathological patterns, these dysfunctional patterns at times became very nebulous to the families themselves. The dysfunctional patterns at some point started to be seen as part of Native American tradition. Since people were forced to assimilate white behaviors—many of which were inherently dysfunctional—the ability to differentiate healthy from dysfunctional became difficult (or impossible) for the children who were to become the grownups of the boarding school era. Therefore, many of the problems facing Native American people today—such as alcoholism, child abuse, suicide, and domestic violence—have become part of the Native American heritage due to the long decades of forced assimilation and genocidal practices implemented by the federal government.

The Psychology of the Colonized Native American Male

During the authors' many years of working in a therapeutic context with Native American men, some common themes began to emerge. This section deals with the psychological ramifications of the colonization of the men/warriors. This is not to say that the women do not suffer also, but the psychological process is different and must be analyzed separately. Warriors are supposed to repel the enemy and insure the safety of the community; when this is not possible, defeat has deep psychological ramifications. These ramifications are even greater if the colonizer imposes a diametrically opposed mythology on the people and also on the land that the warriors are supposed to keep safe and alive within the traditional tribal lifeworld. Add to this the destruction of men's role in the traditional economy and you have men divested of meaningful cultural roles.

Once a warrior is defeated and his ability to protect the community destroyed, a deep psychological trauma of identity loss occurs. The roles that were familiar are no longer there, and he becomes alienated within his own internal as well as external worlds. The alienation becomes compounded when the conquering armies become the ongoing colonizers—a constant reminder to the Native American men of the loss of the community. The fact that the conquerors remain is a continual source of aggravation and hostile feelings, which cannot be expressed and therefore are repressed. The repressed feelings of loss and rage then develop a life of their own in the unconscious or in the "black world," where they may not be accessible to the conscious life of the person except through dreams and visions. Nonetheless, the repressed feelings in the "black world" continue to haunt the warrior due to a need for these feelings to become resolved and thus allow the person to regain harmony.

How is it that the warrior psyche that once nurtured the family and community has turned against the loved ones for whom the warrior at one time sacrificed himself? Borrowing from the psychoanalytic and object relations perspectives, we can began to make some sense of this problem. The reader should bear in mind that psychoanalytic perspectives are used here as a vehicle of analysis and are not the only method by which the phenomenon of violence against loved ones can be understood.

When the colonization process is perpetrated in such a savage fashion as was done in the Western Hemisphere, there occurs a splitting of the personality that is consistent with the level of trauma. The feelings of helplessness and hopelessness are compounded to such a degree as to make the choice complete psychosis or splitting of the ego into at least two fragments. The split ego, then, will keep one aspect of the person in touch with the pain and one aspect identifying with the aggressor. It is a well known historical fact that some of the greatest Native American leaders were either betrayed or killed by Native American men who lost themselves in their identification with the aggressor.

Identification with the aggressor at times has a peculiar quality in Native American men, which may not be found in the classic literature of identification with the aggressor. This identification with the aggressor by Native American men is of a quality that has as a core a desire to gain the aggressor's power and eventually turn that power on the aggressor. At a deep level the acquisition of the aggressor's power has the ultimate goal of destroying the aggressor and restoring the community to a precolonization lifeworld. Because removal of the colonial forces is not realized, the repressed rage has no place for cathexis except to turn on itself.

The devastating effects of the internalized cathexis are no secret in Native American country. Suicide rates have been the highest of any ethnic group for decades. In order for the anger to be held in some sort of abeyance, the individual requires an anesthesia. The incidence of alcoholism among Native Americans over the last two hundred years shows the extent to which alcohol has served as a medicine that keeps this rage within some type of boundary.

Alcohol, on the other hand, can serve as a vehicle that removes impulse control and allows for venting of the rage. In order for the cathecting outward of the energy to occur in a way that preserves the physical life of the warrior, the rage is vented on the family. Generations have elapsed during which the lamentations of women and children haunt the landscape in what appears to be the stillness of reservations across the country. It is almost as if women and families have been sacrificing themselves in order to preserve the tattered remains of the warrior tradition. Many wise elders in the Native American community believe that it is the women who have been carrying the traditions in order to ensure that they continue living.

Because women are the ones who carry life, it makes sense that they are the ones who have been carrying the life of the people through their sacrifices over the past five hundred years. The regression of tradition in the male has been based on the male's inability to be physically pregnant. Since humans interpret psychological and spiritual reality through physical perception, the issue of pregnancy or the carrying and giving of life becomes symbolically important. If we accept that males can be psychologically and spiritually pregnant, then we can expect the male to carry and give birth to the spiritual life in the community. The female, through her ability to be pregnant, has gestated the traditional lifeworld in order to ensure its life. Since the female brings into the world the physical life of the people, the expectation has been that she also carries the psychological and spiritual well-being and life of the community. However, this should be a role shared by men and women.

Because of the male's misunderstanding of the female's role, the task of the female has been one of extreme sacrifice, and at times the sacrifice has involved the absorption of the negative cathexis of the repressed male rage. It is important not to jump to the conclusion that Native American women want to get hurt—they do not; their sacrifice is one of ensuring the life of the people through preservation of the warrior archetype. A clear example of the support of the women for the warriors takes place in the Sun Dance ceremony. The women literally stand behind the men to help them undertake the spiritual renewal (rebirth) of the community. Without the combined, shared effort, the men could not withstand the ceremony; the men need the women's support due to the men's inherent weakness and the fact that they can't experience physical childbirth. Symbolically, women have been standing behind the men for a half millennium, and they are fatigued. It has become critical that the men once again undertake the responsibility of providing a life-giving vessel for the well-being of the community. Instead, what we find many times is the male shattering the life-giving vessel via the dysfunction of domestic violence.

Andy Curry has discussed some of the dynamics of internalized rage as he has learned this dynamics from working among rageful black males. Curry states that "the explicit and conscious act of killing involves the affirmation of life, which is nourished by that which is killed. . . . Death belongs to life, perhaps not as specifically as the phrase 'destructive love' suggests. But they are nevertheless related. The patient has not actually committed murder; he is, we may quickly conclude, only killing an image of himself" (1972, p. 103). It is not difficult to connect the image of the broken warrior wanting to destroy that image in order to affirm the life of the "true" warrior who has regressed into the unknown of the "black world" or the unconscious.

In order to get a better understanding of these dynamics, the reader must know that shame is of critical concern within a warrior tradition. Shame is akin to existential death, and the split-off segment of the warrior must react to the shame incurred. Curry, eloquently states, "In responding to shame-producing situations such an individual uses a simple remedy: inflict on others the narcissistic injuries which he is most afraid of suffering himself" (1972, p. 77).

The learning and social modeling that were ingrained during the reservation and mission school era arc unmistakable. Warrior children were punished for any behavior that remotely resembled the traditional image. The split ego readily attached to this in order to stop the abuse, and the price was that of internalizing the hate for what was "true" tradition. Again, the cathexis for such a psychosis-producing double bind is to inflict the rage on a part of himself—the family.

As mentioned before, the problem is compounded by the colonizers being a constant reminder of the defeat. The warrior is further split into yet another double bind—being Native American and also living as a white person. The imposing of yet another double bind requires the strongest of medications in order to keep complete dissociation from occurring. Within the medical model, phenothiazines are presently used to sedate the patient; Native Americans have long been using the nonprescription drug alcohol as a way of ensuring survival. Alcohol has become such an integral part of life that many Native Americans no longer dissociate alcohol from what used to be the traditional way of life. The warrior has become someone who can only function within the ceremony of alcohol. The nurturing male has become destructive to the sacred trust that was given to him—the family, community, and relationship with the sacred.

Presently, we find many of our brothers with a fragmented spirituality. They get sober for thirty days and immediately they want to recapture the relationship with the sacred by becoming medicine men. They have truly forgotten that the medicine cannot work outside of an intact family and community context.

This has led to a tradition in which our people place tremendous burden on "true" spiritual leaders as they pressure them for miracles and quick magical fixes for the pain and suffering that never seems to end. It must be noted that the choices given Native American men by the colonists are those of being a drunk Indian or a medicine man. In a way, the modern male continues to internalize the projections of the white society and attempts to recapture that projection instead of going into the black world and recovering the lost warrior who is waiting for conscious contact.

The dynamic of the warrior internalizing and reacting to the lifeworld in a dysfunctional way can be examined through a PTSD paradigm. Posttraumatic stress disorder can be manifested in primary or secondary symptoms. Primary symptoms are those acquired through firsthand account or experience of the trauma. Secondary PTSD is a normal reaction and can be acquired by having family and friends who have been acutely traumatized. These reactive behaviors are passed on and learned and become the norm for subsequent generations. The normal behaviors of the traumatized person have to change in order to deal with the traumatic event.

PTSD has several phases as the disorder evolves from trauma to possible recovery (Peterson, Prout and Schwarz 1991). The model offered here has been modified to make it relevant to Native American populations:

l. Impact or Shock. The first phase starts at the moment the person is traumatized. As mentioned in the theoretical discussion above, this is the point at which the ego must split in order to avoid complete dissociation. There is either a partial or complete regression, which allows the complex to develop a life of its own in the unconscious. Lack of resolution of the repressed issues are continuously manifested in symptoms that require some type of medication. If the person does not medicate him/herself, then the only defense left in the light of pain is dissociation. The person no longer has an awareness of who or where s/he is, thus rendering them nonexistent.

2. Withdrawal and Repression (Warrior Regression). At this point, the person attempts to survive psychologically in the only way available to him/her. One of the quickest ways to psychologically survive is to withdraw emotionally and literally shut down emotions so as to avoid the pain. The warrior archetype is thereby withdrawn from the world, leaving an emptiness in the life of the person, family, and community. Attempts by the archetype to make itself manifest are plagued with unknown problems, which are for the most part expressed in a nonconstructive way. Native American men have a high enlistment rate into the military and usually serve in a "beyond the call of duty" manner. By serving as a warrior the traditional warrior has some expression, except that the man is serving as a warrior protecting the way of life of the people who have destroyed his traditional way of life. Serving in the colonial army can only contribute to the dissonance and splitting that the Native American male is already experiencing.

3. Acceptance/Repression (Magical Thinking). This phase is characterized by denial; the person attempts to believe that things are not as bad as they seem or that they will get better through some miraculous intervention. There have been many instances in the history of the colonization process where Native American people thought that if they were to have just the "right type" of medicine that a way of life would magically be restored. That ideology persists to this day. Many of our brothers and sisters who find themselves plagued by some of the problems already related in this book believe that if they perform some ritual all will be taken care of. They seem to have forgotten that what gives medicine its effectiveness is the cohesive community. Without community cohesion the medicine loses its power. The fact that so many people claim to be Traditional and continue to maintain dysfunctional lifestyles is another infraction that dilutes the power of the medicine.

4. Compliance and Anger (Decompensation). The person at this point realizes that things are going to continue to be bad and that optimism is unrealistic. This creates a sense of anger, and at times the rage is ambivalent. The person cannot cathect the rage and does not know at whom the rage needs to be targeted. In many instances the anger is targeted against members of the family. This is the point at which the internalized self-hate creates ego-splitting, as in the dynamics discussed above.

5. Trauma Mastery (Healing). This is the ideal final stage at which the person hopefully arrives. Through understanding of the dynamics of the trauma, the person finally validates their reality and focuses the anger and frustration at the appropriate target. At this point the person realizes that s/he, the family, and the tribe are the victims of a scenario that was initiated over one hundred years ago. Methods of healing are discussed below.

Without the awareness of some of these dynamics, it is very difficult for a practitioner working with Native American people to be effective. Through ignorance, most practitioners continue to invalidate the experience of trauma in Native American people, which in turn becomes an ongoing infliction of trauma on the patient. The Native American patient already feels decades of horrendous unresolved grief and rage, and the practitioner adds to this through the insensitivity of blaming the victim by pathologizing clients, as is so common in Western psychotherapy. Such iatrogenics perpetrates the suffering.

Loss of Initiation Ritual and Ramifications

One of the devastations of the colonization process for Native Americans has been the systematic destruction of the initiation ceremony. Even though some tribes retain some of these ceremonies, many tribes do not, and this fact contributes to the problems facing the modern Native American male—especially in the modern lifeworld. Females are more fortunate because even though they may not have a formal ritual, natural processes have a way of performing the initiation for them.

Once more we have a double bind situation for Native American youths who are about to become adults. They need the guidance and ceremony to launch them into adulthood, but there are few and in some places no grownups who can deal with the issues of initiation in a positive fashion. As everyone knows, this is not enough to stop the developmental process. Therefore, an initiation takes place, except that the initiation is one which emerges out of the unknown and for the most part is one which keeps the individual struggling with the ongoing intergenerational PTSD. When there is no ritual prescribed by the community, rituals from colonial sectors.

Recently we have seen Native American adolescents involved in substance/alcohol abuse, gangs, or satanic and other cult activities. This can be interpreted as the youths searching for some group to help them with their journey from adolescence to adulthood. As part of the drug culture Native American youths are offered an initiation into a community that at least on the surface provides existential meaning and relief for their pain. In initiation ceremonies and preparation the youths used to get instruction as to how to deal with the different entities and realms of good and evil. Presently, the only instruction our youths get in the area of evil is the fearful reaction of adults via organized Western religion.

Initiation has a different effect on males than on females. Even though a female might not have a ceremony proper, she still undergoes a physical initiation at the time of menstruation. At this time, she knows that there is an interconnectedness between herself and the cyclical nature of life. The initiation she undergoes is complete with the pain and bleeding that are an integral part of male initiation rituals in most cultures. The problem in modern Western culture is that the young girl is then made to feel dirty or unclean because of her cyclical relationship with the Earth.

The young boy is not so fortunate in his initiation by nature. Even though there are the physiological changes that occur through puberty, there is no ritual that as clearly defines him as a man as the menstrual event does a young woman. The boy must learn what he can from the talk of other uninitiated boys and men. There are no warriors to initiate him into the mysteries and responsibilities of the warrior tradition. What the young boy learns about being a man is what he sees on television or what he is exposed to at home. Unfortunately, in most cases the boy sees only behavior that is not nourishing to the family, and the media convinces him that the destructive traits of the male are the ones that are held in high esteem by the society. The situation has become increasingly cyclical and complex, since in order to initiate others the adult must have undergone some initiation himself. The history of family breakdown and dysfunction indicates that this cannot happen, since instead of the initiation ceremony, Native Americans have inherited several generations of unresolved trauma.

The therapist must understand that until recently Native American people had a culture that abounded with the resources needed for a harmonious existence. The Native American person was a human being trying to understand and live in peace within his/her cosmological reality. Special care must be taken at this point not to confuse this idea with the image of the noble savage. The noble savage projection is when a Native American is seen as someone who is a mystical being who can do magic and other spiritual tasks, but is not too adept at thinking things through in a day-to-day existence. This fantasy material is portrayed in the media and carried into the therapeutic session by many Western therapists. Native Americans had a very well structured society in which everyone's role and place was well defined. Our family systems and self-governance supported these roles and functions, and everyone felt valued as a member of the community.

Holistic worldviews such as the one expressed above allowed Native American people to experience the world as a totality of which they were an integral part. This experience does not necessarily imply that Native Americans were completely immersed in "participation mystique" (the notion that there is little or no ego differentiation and the individual cannot determine a sense of self and merely sees him/herself as a part of the world), as some anthropologists have speculated. This holistic worldview allowed Native Americans to have a unified awareness or perception of the physical, psychological, and spiritual phenomena that make up the totality of human existence or consciousness. In the experience of such a unified awareness, there was also a close integration with cosmological realities as they were experienced or perceived.

Native American people were able to have a centered awareness that was fluid and nonstatic. The centered awareness allowed for a harmonious attitude toward the world, as exemplified by a tribal collective way of life versus an individualistic approach. The harmony idea is best illustrated by the acceptance and being part of the mystery of existence versus the ongoing struggle to understand the world through a logical positivistic approach, as exemplified by Western science.

The core of Native American awareness was the place where the soul wound occurred. This core essence is the fabric of soul and it is from this essence that mythology, dreams, and culture emerge. Once the core from which soul emerges is wounded, then all of the emerging mythology and dreams of a people reflect the wound. The manifestations of such a wound are then embodied by the tremendous suffering that the people have undergone since the collective soul wound was inflicted half a millennium ago. Some of the diseases and problems that Native American people suffer are a direct result of the soul wound. These self-destructive behaviors may be a desperate attempt to bring back a harmonious soul. This issue receives more theoretical analysis in chapter 4.

Dreams as a Vehicle

Since the unconscious and the manifestations of the unconscious are accessible to both traditional and orthodox Western approaches, it is reasonable to ascertain that dreams can be a vehicle to help in the healing and integration of world cosmologies. Since the soul wound occurred at the level of myth and dream, it follows that the therapy or transformation of the wound should also occur at the level of myth and dream. The level at which the wound occurred is accessible through the vehicle of dreams, since dreams are part of the awareness that emerges from the depths of the unconscious. Dreams have had an important role to all peoples; perhaps this commonality can serve as the thread that we can use in order to sew the tear that has occurred in the psyche of both Western and non-Western peoples. Attention has been devoted to the dreams of primitive peoples by anthropologists, and those anthropological interests fall into three categories: ethnographic, historical, and psychoanalytic. The ethnologist investigates how dreams may be the source for general assumptions of the nature of the world, while the cultural anthropologist may use a more psychoanalytic system for dream interpretation.

As early as 1668 there was documentation as to the importance of dreams in Native American culture. The Jesuits found that the Iroquois religion was largely based on dream phenomena as a guide for all important occurrences in life. Father Fermin wrote:

> The Iroquois have, properly speaking, only a single divinity—the dream. To it they render their submission and follow all its orders with the utmost exactness. The Tsonnontouens (Seneca) are more attached to their superstition than any of the others; their religion in this respect become even a matter of scruple; whatever it be that they think they have done in their dreams, they believe themselves absolutely obliged to execute at the earliest moment. The other nations content themselves with observing those dreams which are the most important; but this people, which has the reputation of living more religiously than its neighbors, would think itself guilty of a great crime if it failed in its observance of a single dream. The people think only of that, and all their cabins are filled with their dreams. (Wallace 1958, p. 236)

It is apparent that differences in worldviews are present in the above observation. As discussed earlier, separation of religion or spirituality and the psychological reality does not exist for Native Americans, as it does for Westerners. Within Native American traditions, the healer also serves as the priest and psychotherapist and not only helps people stay in balance within the earthly context, but also helps the individual understand and stay in accord with the sacred dimension of existence.

In Western philosophy there has not always been a split between the soul and body. In the early Greek traditional healings of the followers of Asklepius, the healing worldview was very similar to that of Native American people. The priest acted as the healer and conduit of the god Asklepius himself through the ritual of the healing ceremony. It was not until later, through the Hippocratic tradition, that the split began to emerge in Western healing. Via classical thinkers such as Socrates, the split was made complete. The split in Western consciousness was reaffirmed and made even more explicit by the philosophy of René Descartes, who shattered the remaining Western psyche with his monumental cogito crgo sum (I think, therefore I am). This statement illustrates the Western notion of separation of mind and body and is the basis of the subject-object debate.

The main vehicle of healing in the Asklepian tradition, as in the Native American tradition, was the dream. After a purification ceremony the priest would take the patient into an inner chamber, where the patient would go to sleep and have a healing dream, with Asklepius accomplishing the healing. This healing method of treatment is very closely related to many Native American traditional approaches in which the priest helps in the purification of the patient, who is then "doctored" by healing spirits. For this reason, E.D.'s work over the past decade in Native American country has involved the use of dreamwork in all contexts of clinical practice. The dream vehicle has opened up avenues where none existed and has allowed many patients to come in contact with their own healing. We discuss clinical work further in part 2.

Very early on, the Native American tradition employed systems of analysis for dream material. According to A. F. Wallace, the Iroquois used a system resembling psychoanalysis. As far back as 1646, Father Ragueneau described the analytic system as follows:

> In addition to the desires which we generally have that are free, or at least voluntary in us, (and) which arise from a previous knowledge of some goodness that we imagine to exist in the thing desired, the Hurons (and, he might have

added, the Seneca) believe that our souls have other desires, which are, as it were, inborn and concealed. These, they say, come from the depths of the soul, not through any knowledge, but by means of a certain blind transporting of the soul to certain objects; these transports might in the language of philosophy be called *Desideria innata*, to distinguish them from the former, which are called *Desideria elicita*. (Wallace 1958, p. 238)

Although there are what appear to be psychoanalytic traces within this system due to considerations of desires within the interpretation of dreams, the Iroquois interpretation system goes beyond wish fulfillment. The notion of inborn and concealed depths of the soul is without a doubt beyond the realm of psychoanalysis and its notions of wish fulfillment. Instead, these inborn traits are qualities of the dream and are more closely associated with the concepts of the collective unconscious as described by Jung. However, it is difficult to credit Jung with a concept that was already old in 1646.

The dream therapy of Native Americans was used in a healing context and was instrumental in the selection and initiation of shamans and priests. When an individual was to become a shaman among the Eskimo, dreams were an important phase of the initiation. When the Shaman Iyjugarjuk was very young he was visited constantly by dreams that he could not understand. Beings of unknown places came and spoke to him, and he told his people about his dreams. Because of his dreams it became accepted that Iyjugarjuk was to become a shaman and an initiatory process was commenced (Campbell 1979). Among the Apache, supernatural power could also be obtained from a dream or a hallucinatory experience. The dream was used as a messenger of power from another realm that allowed the individual to experience the sacred in a way that was initiatory in nature.

D. Handelman discussed the development of the last shaman of the Washo Native Americans of western Nevada and eastern California:

During his early years Henry (shaman) had a series of dreams which he still remembers with clarity, and which probably marked him early as having shamanic and mystic potential. As he describes the situation, he would go to sleep on the ground inside the family lean-to and dream of a bear who came and stood in the lean-to opening and stared at him. When he looked at the bear it would vanish, and then Henry would fly up into the sky toward the moon. In 1902 Henry experienced his power dream, which marked him as a shaman: I was sleeping in the school dormitory. I had a dream. I saw a buck in the west. It was a horned buck. It looked east. A voice said to me: don't kill my babies any more. I woke up, and it was raining outside, and I had a nosebleed in bed. (1976, p. 381)

Further uses of dreams have been documented by E. W. Gifford among the Northfork Mono. In his accounts he discussed a specialized healer called a soahuhiere (talker). The function of the talker was to drive out a spirit that had appeared in a dream and made the dreamer ill. The method of removing the illness caused by a dream was to sing before the patient, shake a cocoon rattle, go out to consult the spirits, return putting ashes on the head of the sick person, and blow them from him and proceed to announce the cure.

At times these people dreamed that they were sick and certain songs were sung by the talker to cure the illness. The afflicted person informed the shaman of his dreams, and the shaman talked to the guilty spirit at night, outdoors, asking the spirit to cease making the person sick.

Dream work is an ancient practice that is a part of the earliest experiences of humanity. The following account given by Gifford is evidence of the importance of dreams in a past that can only be recaptured by messages left by way of a pictograph on the side of a cave wall:

The Northfork Mono were firm believers in the significance of dreams. A pictograph in a cave four miles east of Fuller's meadow Madera county, was said to depict a man's dreams.

Dreams did not always make one a shaman, however, as the following instance indicates: an informant dreamed about a coyote. A few days later the exact events of the dream were enacted. As she was walking along a road, a large coyote suddenly sprang out and rolled on his back in the dust before her, his tongue out. Then he got up and trotted ahead of her for a distance, continually looking back. Suddenly he disappeared. The woman consulted a soahuhiere shaman, who told her she should not have thought about the dream, for by doing so she made it come true. (1932, p. 52)

The notion of living out dreams is a cross-tribal phenomenon. There are rules and taboos about reporting dreams, which makes the discussion of dreams a concern for the Western therapist who is naive to this practice. The therapist must become informed as to the different rules of reporting and discussing dreams within the tribal context in which s/he is working.

Other aspects of life that were affected by the dreamtime included the establishment of taboos and the giving of songs. In one instance a girl could not eat rabbit because the taboo was given to her by dreaming and if she ate rabbits her children would kick like rabbits. The shaman who might be in need of more power in order to continue his doctoring duties would receive such power through an animal dream helper. The animal appearing in a dream would speak to its protégé, saying "use me," or something of that nature, and would give the individual a song. If the individual chosen to have power accepted the offered power, he took care not to forget the song and sought another experience with the dream helper. Further instructions were given to the person by the dream helper in later encounters, and other songs were given at these times.

According to Gayton, at times the dream might come to someone who was not intentionally seeking power. No one was obliged to take a dream. Many people felt that the rules of fasting, praying in an isolated spot, taking a tobacco emetic, basking in the sun, and so on, which were necessary to a successful relationship with the occult, were too troublesome. Others were afraid of attempting it lest they make a mistake and incur the ill will of the dream creature. Relatively few persons, and these only men, became professional shamans. The amount of power that a shaman possessed, according to Gayton, was also in direct proportion to the dreams: "It was merely a greater quantity, and accumulation of dream experience, say six, to an average person's of two. The more of such experience one had the greater his knowledge of the occult would become, and the bond between the individual and the supernatural world increasingly strengthened" (1930, p. 389).

There is ample ethnographic evidence of the importance of dreams and associated phenomena among Native American people. E.D.'s work with Native American people in the last few years indicates that dreams are still a very important part of daily life. The importance of dreams spans daily mundane life, healing, and relating to the sacred plane of existence. It is not advisable to focus on dreams as simply a therapeutic tool and ignore the integral part that the dream plays in the overall life of the individual and group.

In Western psychology dreams have also played a very important role. Freud's monumental contribution to science was followed by Jung and a plethora of theory and clinical techniques focusing on dream interpretation. Not only has Western psychology focused on the clinical application of dream interpretation, but much research has also been done on physiological as well as psychological aspects of dreaming. What we have, then, is an entity common to all cultures that allows psychologists from different worldviews to begin the bridge-building process. Perhaps psychology, with its emphasis on physical science, has gone in a different direction from the traditional healers, but this need not constitute an uncrossable barrier.

We are convinced that once we start dealing with some of these issues we will be able contribute to meaningful cross-cultural applications. In no way do we want to imply even for an instant that Western therapists can become shamans, as the pop literature may indicate. Rather, we attempt to facilitate an open dialogue between the traditions and pave the way for a new cooperative research, clinical, and healing effort.

Conclusions

Attempts have been made to discuss healing from perspectives that bridge the colonized personal experience by using analytic systems of both the colonized and colonizer. The task seems to be doomed from the beginning, since by looking through the lens of the colonizer and his systems of critique, we only continue the hegemonic process experienced by the colonized. As well, this situation is not helped by the use of the English language in presenting the discussion. The authors believe that there can be an integrated system of analysis that lends itself to a discourse that need not be hegemonic to either tradition, and may actually be liberating for both.

Some of the notions discussed in this chapter may be seen as strange and outside the paradigm of Western psychology. For the authors to have maintained a Western outlook would have merely contributed to the epistemic violence from which Native American communities have been suffering for many generations. Western thinkers must acknowledge that there are legitimate forms of generating knowledge in the native community and this knowledge is valid in its own right, standing alongside that of other cosmologies. Western psychology is in desperate need of explanations for the illnesses that plague society in general; presently, the Western system of disease conceptualization and treatment is inadequate. A clear indication of this inadequacy is the constant changing of the diagnostic criteria as found in the DSM-II, III, III-R, and now the DSM-IV. We feel certain the DSM-IV will not be the final word on diagnosis; the fifth edition is probably being written even as this book finds its way to the reader.

If the Western categorization of illness is falling short of the mark in the white community, these categories must obviously fall much shorter when applied to the native client. In the future it will be beneficial to Native American people if the diagnostic manual takes into account some of the issues presented in this book. Many Native American people are diagnosed based on erroneous criteria; the diagnostic process never takes a historical perspective in the placing of a diagnosis on the client. The authors fantasize that one day the DSM-III will have diagnostic criteria such as "acute or chronic reaction to genocide and colonialism." Until that day comes there will be little honesty from the Western healing traditions in their relationships with Native Americans, and the ongoing ethnocide will continue under the guise of Western healing. Unless Western systems—which belong to the power brokers—began to accept non-Western forms of knowledge as legitimate, Western therapy will continue to be impotent.

The legitimization of Native American thought in the Western world has not yet occurred, and may not occur for some time. This does not mean that the situation is hopeless in the Native American community. The Native American community can help itself by legitimizing its own knowledge and thus allowing for healing to emerge from within the community. If the perpetrators prefer to live in denial, that is an issue with which they will have to deal presently and historically. Clinically, once the pathology is cured in one area of the system, another area of the system will begin to show symptoms. Presently, there is a lot of healing happening in the Native American community; who is beginning to lurk around the periphery and want some of the healing from the Native Americans? The perpetrators, tired of living with a mythology that is no longer applicable, appear thirsty for these indigenous forms of healing and are willing to pay money for them. Little do they know that the only price that will purchase healing for them is historical honesty.

4

Theoretical Concerns

In the beginning of all things, wisdom and knowledge were with the animals; for Tirawa, the One Above, did not speak directly to man. He sent certain animals to tell men that he showed himself through the beasts, and that from them, and from the stars and the sun and the moon, man should learn. Tirawa spoke to man through his works.

—Chief Letakots-Lesa

Centering the Therapist and Shamanic Parallels

Many of the counseling approaches of the past few decades have been influenced by Carl Rogers's notion of client-centered therapy. The therapist that does this form of therapy usually focuses the intervention on the client's capacity to more fully encounter reality" (1942). The therapeutic change or growth is accomplished through the relationship with the therapist who acts as the empathic agent of change. According to Rogers, the therapist must also provide an environment conducive to becoming a fully functioning person.

The role of the therapist is one in which s/he should be without a role as much as possible. According to Rogers, the therapist should be able and willing to enter the client's world; this act loosens the client's defense mechanisms to a point which will allow higher functioning. The therapeutic change occurs when the incongruence between reality and the client's perception is resolved and the adjustment is made psychologically, thus allowing the client to change and to ameliorate the struggle.

One of the notions that is not commonly referred to within the Rogerian system is that the therapist's attitudes and genuineness has power in the therapy. Crucial to the issues discussed in this section is the idea of therapist-centered therapy as explored in a cross-cultural context. A comparison and integration with shamanic approaches are attempted in order to yield an approach in which the therapist becomes more cognizant of his/her power and the responsibility in the use of such power.

Among some groups of people of non-Western worldviews, the focus of the therapeutic encounter is on the healer or therapist. Societies that adhere to a shamanic approach to therapy have difficulty with the notion of the patient or client being the center of therapy as in the Rogerian system. According to M. Sandner, some of the rituals associated with shamanic practice are evidence that the power and the healing symbolism is carried by the shaman (1979, p. 259).

Some of the similarities between the Western and traditional approaches have been delineated by Donald Sandner, a

Jungian analyst in San Francisco. These similarities are not accidental, and the role of the therapist must be very clear; this clarity can be achieved "by strictly defining the position of the man who will plunge him into a powerful imagery, and render him extremely vulnerable" (1979, p. 100). Sandner believes that the effectiveness of psychotherapy depends more on what we do than on what we know, therapy process being more important than the content of the words spoken or the quantifiable objective world.

In the traditional notion of therapy, the veracity of the healing process is not contingent on objective reality. According to the renowned anthropologist Claude Lévi-Straus:

> That the mythology of the shaman does not correspond to objective reality does not matter. The patient believes in it and belongs to a society that believe in it. The protecting spirits, the evil spirits, and supernatural monsters and magical monsters are elements of a coherent system which are the basis of the natives' concept of the universe. The patient accepts them or rather she never doubted them. What she does not accept are the incomprehensible and arbitrary pains which represent an element foreign to her system but which the shaman, by invoking the myth, will replace in a whole in which everything has its proper place. (1958, p. 217)

The shaman, psychotherapist, and medicine man have roles that are clearly defined in their respective traditions. Even though the objective of all three traditions is to produce harmony and cure illness, the means to those ends vary. Sandner gives a good description of the method or technique of each respective practice:

1. The shaman enacts the symbolism in his own person through periods of ecstatic trance. S/he alone is the carrier and focus of symbolic power; the patient is only a passive participant who must go along with the shaman.

2. The Navajo medicine man does not act out the symbolism in his own person. He remains impassive and reserved, and the main focus of the symbolic action is presented to the patient through songs, prayers, and sand paintings. The medicine man draws upon a vast body of traditional symbolism, but he does not live it out.

3. In the psychotherapist mode or method of healing the doctor is comparatively passive. Not only are there no ecstatic journeys, but neither are there dancing, singing, sandpainting, or any of the other culturally prescribed activities of the first two modes. There is no large traditional body of symbolism for the doctor to draw upon for the benefit of the patient. The main focus of the symbolic action is from the patient him/herself. (1959, p. 259–261)

Even though there are differences in the approaches to treatment, some of these differences can be reconciled. If it serves the interest of the patient, particularly in a cross-cultural context, then the therapist must be flexible and at least make an attempt to meet the patient within his/her own worldview. According to Sandner:

in any discussion of neurotic manifestations, whether in preliterate or literate societies, attention must be paid to the cultural or subcultural variables. While family and interpersonal experiences from birth are what give neurosis its degree of presence in an individual, culture gives it form and social context. The family and the individual are immersed in culture as a fish in the ocean. Decades of anthropology have shown that culture is in the bone; objectivity is an illusion when it comes to viewing one culture from the standpoint of another. (1979, p. 97)

Sandner leaves very little to interpretation in this statement, especially when it comes to the impossibility of objectivity in the therapeutic context. Sandner is cautioning the therapist as to the attention that must be paid to the culture of the client who is involved in the therapeutic encounter. Most therapists would do well to honestly scrutinize their cross-cultural blind spots; by so doing, the quality of therapy can be greatly enhanced.

Even the dreams of patients are affected by the cultural strata of the psyche. Hersch believes that there are dreams which may be "pure expressions of a particular culture." These dreams "seem to carry the spirit of a people in such a way that the whole mood or atmosphere of the dream is more important than any particular symbol. It is a mistake, therefore, to examine the symbols of these dreams primarily as expressions of cross-cultural archetypes, even though the symbols may be of a collective nature" (1980, p. 183).

A comparison of Western therapy with shamanism has yielded some interesting findings which illustrate that all of the effective components found in psychotherapy are also an integral part of shamanic healing. B. Moody found in his comparative study (1987) that many factors are similar in the two different therapeutic camps.

Therapists and shamans use the method of suggestion as part of the therapeutic encounter. Both the therapist and the shaman behave in such a way as to suggest to the patient that their "medicine" will help bring relief to the patient's suffering. The fact that most therapists charge a substantial amount of money is suggestive that the patient is buying something of value. Even though most therapists insist that they do not promise anything to their patients, they rarely deny that they do try to alleviate suffering—or at least give meaning to it. The shaman is not as timid as the therapist in this regard. The community will not stand for a shaman who does not return lost souls or facilitate some sort of cure with the patients s/he sees.

Prognostic expectation is an important factor in the therapeutic process. This factor is easy to document among therapy-goers; long distances were traveled by people all over the world in order to have Freud or Jung as their analyst. The same is true with shamanism, and if there is a powerful shaman who has built a powerful reputation, then clients will travel great distances to be seen by that shaman. In this sense, the expectation of the client greatly facilitates the treatment.

The expectation that the patient has of the role of the healer has also been found to relate to favorable outcome in both psychotherapy and shamanism. The role of the healer is defined by the culture, and the healer acts powerfully as s/he lives out the role of healer in day-to-day life.

Emotional arousal is a technique that is useful in all therapeutic work. High arousal is associated with a more favorable therapeutic outcome. Shamans use dancing, drumming, and chanting to accomplish this arousal, whereas Western therapists use guided imagery, which can be associated with shamanic ecstasy.

One of the crucial notions of shamanism is that the unconscious or the spirit of the healer is of critical importance to the therapeutic encounter. Western therapy describes this phenomenon in the construct of countertransference. According to Jung (1954), during therapy the therapist must at all times be vigilant over his/her own unconscious processes. If the therapist ignores his/her own unconscious, then the patient may suffer disastrous effects from the therapeutic encounter. The therapist must be in a constant state of awareness as the therapy is conducted and also after the client leaves. Since the therapeutic encounter affects the unconscious of the therapist as well as the unconscious of the patient, the therapist, through having awareness of his/her own dreams, can also safeguard the therapeutic process.

The phenomenon of countertransference has been one with which non-Western cultures have dealt for hundreds of years, yet psychology has only recently conceptualized its dynamics. Shamans historically were aware of the effects of countertransference and at times would actually consciously engage in the negative use of countertransference. Shamans have long been aware that the ego inflation that results in any type of transference relationship may manifest itself in a positive or negative fashion and the resultant effect is one in which power can be used effectively. The collective power with which the shaman identifies can only occur if the shaman's ego becomes inflated.

The shaman will become an exaggeratedly "good" or "demonic" healer, thus is able to impact the patient both consciously and unconsciously.[1] This process is one in which psychotherapists also engage, except that when they engage in such activities they are less conscious of the process or are utilizing a denial defense mechanism.

Positive inflation sounds innocent enough, except that in reality the therapist does not personify the "good" aspect of the healer archetype. Because of the collective nature of the archetype, the therapist is but a mere speck within the totality of the unconscious and cannot possibly live up to the actual archetypal situation. If the therapist does not move the transference to an objective reality, very little therapy can occur, since the therapist will be overtaken by the moment of pretense and self-adoration.

Instances of the healer's negative inflation abound in ethnographic and oral tradition accounts, as well as in journal accounts about therapists who have hurt their patients. The "bad" shaman at times became inflated in that s/he wanted to demonstrate more power than his/her fellow shamans. In order to demonstrate power superiority, the competitive shaman tries to hurt more people or some people more seriously than his fellow shamans do. In order to deal with these inflated shamans, chiefs had the authority to order their deaths if the negative outweighed the positive for that particular shaman. Unlike shamanic tradition, when a therapist acts in a way that hurts his/her patients, the usual result is that the governing licensing body refers the bad therapist to see another therapist, who may him/herself be good or bad.

In the shamanic tradition of Californian Native Americans, there have been some detailed accounts of negative practices by shamans. According to Gayton:

> This shaman was young and wanted to prove his power. Josie's husband had been working up at Kingston where Pokoi'ik lived. The shaman asked him for some money. He refused, saying that he had no money, that Josie had it all.

---

1. "Inflation" refers to the process in which the ego begins to identify with the archetype or with the spiritual force guiding it.

This was true for the couple had been working hard and saved all they could. Gut Pokoi'ik got mad. He told this old man, "They'll dig up their money when the girl gets sick." He didn't go to Josie to ask for the money but just made Muku-yik sick. He killed her just to prove that he was able to. Said Josie, "Doctors often did this; they just like to try it like we'd try anything."

Pokoi'ik became more malicious as his power increased, and people feared him more. Once Josie's brother, Wepis, and her cousin went up to a fandango given by the Wuk-chumni. Pokoi'ik walked up to Wepis and said, "Do you want to die or do you want to live?" He had been making a practice of doing this, and people had to pay him for fear of losing their lives. . . . When the boys were on the way home a weird, invisible object made of hair frightened the horse which the two boys were riding. Pokoi'ik had sent it. The horses reared, fell backwards, and crushed Josie's cousin. He died before the night was over.

Pokoi'ik finally died. Somebody poisoned him. (1930, p. 396)

The above example is an extreme one, but it is safe to assume that in the beginning the shaman probably started out with the best of intentions. Similar stories can be told about Western therapists and how destructive they can become even though they too started with the best of intentions in helping people.

According to Moody (1987), the ability to channel and control power in therapy is a needed process if therapy is to occur. Rogers (1942) presents a paradoxical use of power in Western therapy, where the client has the right to make choices and the therapist must also be a catalyst in the therapeutic relationship. The Western therapist works by giving up power, thus allowing the client to become empowered. Shamanism, on the other hand, does not struggle with the power paradox. The shaman is per- ceived as powerful within his/her community, and the power that is enacted in the ritual engulfs the client and the shaman in a powerful experience in which the cure occurs. The important difference between the Western therapist's notion of power and that of the shaman is how the power is used. Rather than a controlling or authoritarian use of power, the shaman simply acts powerfully. The perception of power is developed through the belief in the shaman's healing powers such as shamanic journeys and the use of altered states of consciousness. Therefore, the shaman has solved the power issue by not being authoritarian—by not taking away the client's choices, for example. Power becomes a focal point for the mobilization of the client's self-healing powers and also enhances the patient's sense of power through association with the powerful healer. The shaman does not accumulate power for simple personal gain; if this were to occur, the community would deal with the shaman as discussed earlier. The shaman's accumulation of power is dedicated to the work that s/he is to perform in the healing, finding, and restoration of souls.

Another integral part of the therapist-centered approach of the therapeutic process is one in which the patient is allowed to experience death and rebirth as part of the treatment process. The responsibility for the experience cannot be placed completely on the patient since it may be terrifying and the patient needs to be guided by someone who knows how to navigate through these treacherous waters. In traditional approaches, the shaman takes the responsibility of guiding the patient through this process, whereas in Western approaches, the therapist will not take control or guide the process into a death-rebirth process. A shaman once related to E.D. the differences between Western and shamanic approaches to therapy: "Psychologists take the patient all the way to the edge of the cliff and leave him there. What I do is push him over the cliff and go with him, and stay with him as long as it takes to bring him back" (E.D., personal communication, 1984). The shaman is clearly stating the active role of the shaman versus the passive role of the therapist even when the patient may need to have the death-rebirth myth enacted in their transforming process.

The motif of death-rebirth is found in the individuation process described by analytic psychology. Jung describes the death-rebirth process as a renewal without changing the basic being

(1956), since the essential nature is not changed but parts of the personality are healed, strengthened, or improved (1956). John Perry believes that "death also signifies the coming to the end of a phase in development, and the killing off of a self-image, that is, the sacrifice of the leading image of the central archetype, thus allowing its transformation into a new image" (1976, p. 33). Hillman (1979) believes that the journey to the underworld can be an encounter with death and this can be enacted symbolically through the analytic process.

The aforementioned parallels between psychotherapy and shamanism may start paving the way toward a more centered and integrated approach to modern psychotherapy. Since illness and healing have been a part of the human experience since time immemorial, it is reasonable to think that there may be some useful strategies in the methods used by our predecessors. Many correlational notions have been postulated by all sorts of healers for many centuries; no one has really made the attempt to explain what actually happens at the instant healing occurs. Lack of understanding of the healing phenomenon is especially true in the area of nonphysical sickness or of sickness that may be psychological or spiritual in genesis. Volumes by the hundreds have been written concerning techniques and methods by which to categorize and explain the sicknesses of the spirit, soul, or mind.

The illnesses of the psyche have been in existence for millenniums and their manifestations have not changed much during that time. The only thing that is changing from week to week is the approach that modern psychology uses in its attempts to confront and eradicate soul illness. If therapists do not believe in eradication, then the therapeutic profession should at least attempt to find some meaning for this individual and collective suffering.

The problem of bridging the gaps in worldviews is further compounded by the fact that the world has physically been altered by the advent of technology. Since mythology emerges from the Earth itself, the mythology too has changed. Once the mythology changes, so too does the way in which we relate to the world. An area of change that affects the therapeutic arena is the manner in which this mythological shift has impacted the way that people conceptualize illness and healing.

If illnesses have their genesis in a natural world environment, then it seems reasonable that there are therapeutic interventions available in that natural world. In other words, the demons and spirits that were haunting and causing the problems for our ancestors are probably the same ones that bother us today, with the exception that they may have taken a slightly different form in order to accommodate the current myth. The most popular method of addressing the entities that cause illness in the Western world is through collective anesthesia—which is apparent in the very high incidence of alcoholism and substance abuse in our society.

It is at this point that the therapist must be centered and must carry some of the symbolism that the patient has lost. As therapists, we should have knowledge of the entities that have been in the world for a long time; initially, at least, we should enact enough power to avoid the destruction of our patient. The patient cannot be expected to be centered if s/he is not aware of the illness entities that are causing the suffering. The therapist should at least initially be able to provide a center from which the patient can gain strength that will be useful once s/he is aware of the causes of the suffering. When a patient is suffering from ancient spiritual illness, the worst scenario of which a therapist can be a part is denying the existence of such phenomena and leaving the patient alone to deal with the problem with science as their only tool. The centered-therapist paradigm is one that has been proved useful in the shamanic tradition for thousands of years and should be acknowledged as useful by modern therapists.

Archetypal Theory Made Relevant

Before we proceed into clinical discussion we must discuss some underlying archetypal theoretical constructs in order to have a framework from which to make sense of the clinical interventions discussed. One of the single most important connections made by Jung was that of the universality of some of the images of the so-called New World. Jung discovered that some of the motifs that had existed among the Aztecs and the Mayans were identical to Old World motifs. These similarities are obvious and the parallels too close not to be paid special attention. The notion of diffusion is not a likely explanation for similar motifs between cultures, since up to the time of the Spanish conquest the Christian influence had not existed in the New World. The same motifs emerged out of some deep human source that is common to all people. In this assumption of a common human psychological thread that weaves the human psyche as a single fabric as postulated by Jung is a reasonable explanation. The notion of a collective psyche will be used a priori in order to make the case for a psychological integration that will be relevant for Native American people.

One parallel motif was the crucifixion of divinities. What is of interest here is the costume or the special mask by which the ethnic strata of psyche cloaks the more collective interpretation. For those who are not familiar with Jungian jargon, "collective" is all psychic contents that belong not to one individual but to humankind in general. Archetypes fall in the category of being collective in that they represent a very fundamental idea, one which is difficult to reduce any further. An example of a collective idea being masked by the ethnic strata of psyche is provided by Jung:

> The hanging of the victims on crosses was a religious custom in middle America. Muller mentions the Fejervay manuscript, which has for a tail piece, a cross with a gory divinity hanging in the center. Equally significant is the Palenque Cross. At the top is a bird, on either side two human figures facing the cross, one of them holding out a child for either sacrifice or baptism. The ancient Aztecs are said to have invoked the goddess of grain, by nailing a youth or maiden to the cross every spring and shooting the victim with arrows. The name of the cross signifies tree of our flesh. (1956, p. 263)

Huitzilopochtli was a god who was crucified in Aztec mythology; scholars make comparisons between Huitzilopochtli and the hanging of Odin in Norse mythology. According to Jung, people are inclined to trace these images of Odin to Christian influence, thus posing an argument against the collective nature of the psyche. Jung resurrects his theory simply by asking, But what about Huitzilopochtli? In so asking, Jung is implying that even had there been a Christian influence in the myth of Odin, there could not have been Christian influence in the myth of Huitzilopochtli.

Alchemy is another source of symbolism that is collective and in agreement with images and motifs of sacrificing gods. Jung states, "The killing (mortification) of the King occurs in later alchemy. The King's crown makes him a kind of sun. The motif belongs to the wider context of the sacrifice of the god, which developed not only in the west but also in the east, and particularly in ancient Mexico. There the personifier of Tezcatlipoca was sacrificed at the festival of Toxcatl" (1969, p. 80).

Another instance of collective images can be found in the commonality of symbolic eating of the god as in the Eucharist. Jung states:

> I mean the rites of the Aztecs, and in particularly that of the Teoqualo, "god Eating," as recorded by Fray Bernardino de Sahgun. . . . in this rite, a dough like paste was made out of the crushed and pounded seeds of the prickly poppy (*Argemone Mexicana*) and moulded into the figure of the God Huitzilopochtli, and upon the next day the body of Huitzilopochtli died . . . and when he had died thereupon they broke up his body of . . . dough. His heart was apportioned to Moctezuma. (1958, p. 223)

The psychological significance of the religious rituals and motifs described above is rooted in what appears to be an unconscious need to assimilate god by the person and society. A symbolic and unconscious form of transformation occurs in the psyche as the rituals are enacted consciously. The ritual provides the death-rebirth transformative experience to the person or group; this experience actually transcends the field of temporality and places the event at another point in space/time. The transformative process is usually achieved symbolically, and it is in the transforming process that the ritual of therapist-centered therapeutic process becomes critical.

An excellent description of a transformative process is given by Jung in his discussion of the death of Mondamin as a necessary event in the transformation of Hiawatha:

> The battle in the sunset with the corn god gives Hiawatha new strength necessarily so, because the fight against the paralyzing grip of the unconscious calls forth man's creative powers. . . . Hiawatha wrestles with himself in order to create himself. The struggle again lasts for the mythical three days; and on the fourth day, Mondamin prophesied, Hiawatha conquers him, and Mondamin, yielding up his soul sinks to the ground. In accordance with the latter's wish, Hiawatha buries him in the Earth, his mother, and soon afterwards, young and fresh, the corn sprouts from his grave for the nourishment of mankind. Now the remarkable thing here is that it is not Hiawatha who passes through death and emerges reborn, as might be expected, but the god who undergoes transformation in and through man. It is as though he had been asleep in the "mother," i.e., in Hiawatha's unconscious, and had then been roused and fought with so that he should not overpower his host, but should on the contrary himself experience death and rebirth, and reappear in the corn in a new form beneficial to mankind. (1956, p. 336)

The story of Hiawatha is closely paralleled by the vision of Black Elk (1959, p. 32) in which he says, "And where the bison stood a sacred herb sprang up right where the tree had been in the center of the nation's hoop"—clearly a collective vision of a change in mythology. The above themes are not only referring to the transformation of Hiawatha, but to the complete shift in the mythological structure of a society. Now it would no longer be necessary to subsist on the hunt, as had been the case in most Native American societies. At this point the mythology of Native American people was shifting to one of agriculture. During this shift in mythology, religion or the relationship to the sacred is always closely associated with the immediate world—both inner and outer.

Many of the New World psychological processes are interpreted by Western thinkers as being less conscious than Old World processes. Before assuming that Native Americans were still in the "participation mystique" world, the point of reference (Western) from which the judgment is made must be taken into account. These systems of cognition are so different that it is narcissistic to imply that the Western worldview can adequately explain or even understand what Native American people were conscious or unconscious of at that time. The labeling of "primitive" peoples has only encouraged stereotyping and has increased the gap between the worlds. Stereotyping has led the way for mistrust due to the disrespect that European psychology has had for Native American mythological structures and techniques of dealing with the psyche.

Jung is not completely innocent of some of this cultural hegemony, and at times his thinking can be interpreted as having at least overtones of white supremacy. Jung has been quoted as saying that the white person's psyche can be hindered by simply being around primitives or darker-skinned peoples (1972, p. 14). It is certain that Jungians will come to his defense, but this will only add to the already insulted psyche of the so called primitive, What is needed is honesty in paving the way toward a dialogue that values the non-white cosmological worldview. Reference to Jungian shadow is not made simply to indict Jungian psychology and to throw out the baby with the bath water—we are fully aware of how useful and practical Jung's contributions have been. In fact, one of the fundamental ideas of Jungian thinking is that in order to achieve wholeness there must be an existence of the shadow.

Many of the problems faced by Native American people today may be due to the disappearance of old symbolic forms which have been repressed by the unconscious. This repression was a necessary survival mechanism due to the destruction of the environment. Considering that in just one generation many indigenous peoples have lost their source of food—the land—and their religion, it is little wonder that the mythology has regressed.

The alternative would have been complete loss of all life and existence.

If the evolution of consciousness had followed a natural course of development, the shock of contact with the Western worldview might not have been as severe. Had the evolution of the worlds been allowed a proper space of time and the mythologies been allowed the time to integrate in a natural process, the psyche would not have sustained the amount of trauma that it did. The need for the Native American psyche to remain undisturbed is illustrated in a conversation between a Pueblo Native American and Jung: "The chief says, 'Ah my brother, you will never know the happiness of thinking nothing and doing nothing. This is the most delightful thing there is next to sleep. So we were before birth; and so shall be after death'"(1956, p. 325).

This exchange between Jung and the chief can be interpreted in two ways. Analytic psychology interprets the exchange as a need for the chief to remain unconscious. Another approach to the interpretation that is more in line with Native American cosmology is to explain the exchange as the chief telling Jung that it is important to stop the mind, as in Buddhist teaching. By stopping the mind the person is then able to be aware of the world as it really is and not as we wish it to be through our own projective mechanisms. This explanation makes sense, especially as in that same passage Jung says that a chief told him, "the Americans were mad because they were so restless." The problem of trying to figure out the differences in worldviews and how to best perform the *heirosgamos* (holy marriage) of these worldviews and make them accessible to Westerners can perhaps best be accomplished through the typological constructs of Jung.

Figure 1 is a graphical representation of the four Jungian types as seen in two dimensions. The additional two functions would be represented in three-dimensional space and would correspond to extroversion and introversion. According to Jung (1971), these attitudes or types are the basic structures of the personality and they do not need to be static within any given individual. Throughout the individual's life these types will change and shift depending on how the individual decides to

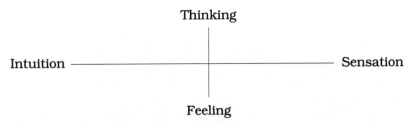

Figure 1. This illustrates Jung's types as he described the four major functions of the psyche. These types can also be affected by extroversion and introversion. Figure constructed by graphically representing Jung's constructs as discussed in Psychological Types, 1971.

evolve these functions, although the individual usually retains a certain attitude predisposed by his/her typology.

According to Jung (1971), the thinking function is "a rational function, because it arranges the contents of ideation under concepts in rational norm of which I am conscious" (p. 481). Opposite the thinking function is the feeling function, which "is primarily a process that takes place between the ego and a given content, a process, moreover, that imparts to the content a definite value in the sense of acceptance or rejection (like or dislike)" (p. 434).

In the horizontal plane we have the opposing functions of intuition and sensation. Jung defines intuition as "a content presents itself whole and complete, without our being able to explain or discover how this content came into existence" (p. 453). Sensation on the other pole is defined as "the psychological function that mediates the perception of physical stimulus. It is therefore, identical with perception. . . . Primarily, therefore, sensation is a sense perception—perception mediated by the sense organs and 'body senses'" (p. 462).

The two functions of introversion and extroversion are usually found in conjunction with these four functions. The possibility of permutations of functions is therefore vast, and this discussion will only address the basic principles of Jung's typology. The introverted function according to Jung is "an inward-turning of libido in the sense of a negative relation of subject to object. Everyone whose attitude is introverted thinks, feels, and acts in a way that clearly demonstrates that the subject is the prime motivating factor and that the object is of secondary importance" (1971, p. 452). In the extroverted attitude we find the opposite process occurring. Jung describes this process as "Everyone in the extroverted state thinks, feels, and acts in relation to the object, and moreover in a direct and clearly observable fashion, so that no doubt can remain about this positive dependence on the object. In a sense, therefore, extroversion is a transfer of interest from subject to object" (1971, p. 427) or an outward turning of libido.

Differences in worldviews may be understood through the diagram in figure 1 and discussion of Jung's types. The Western psyche is more of a thinking type and perhaps places a heavier emphasis on sensation, as is obvious in the way that Westerners are always trying to change the physical world. The attitude within the thinking function is one of a masculine nature, and the masculine attitude idea is useful in understanding the relationship of Westerners with non-Westerners, who may have a more feminine cosmology. The thinking and sensation functions that predominate in Western worldviews are also tempered by a more extroverted approach, thus making the Western mind-set very difficult for the non-Western person to understand.

Since the thinking, sensation, and extroverted attitudes pervade the Western psyche, the introverted, feeling, and intuitive functions, become the inferior functions according to the Western worldview. The inferior function according to Jung is "the function that lags behind in the process of differentiation. The demands of society compel a man to apply himself first and foremost to the differentiation of the function with which he is best equipped by nature, or which will secure him the greatest social success" (1971, p. 450). The functions that remain inferior can also become a source for neurosis, which forces the individual to work toward differentiating these inferior functions.

The fact that Westerners are extroverted also makes their reality more of a so-called objective reality than a subjective one. Even the beginning student can see the disparity in systems; to impose one system of thought over another is very difficult without the input of or discussion with the differing worldview. The reader must refrain from value judgments at this point—it is not a matter of one worldview being better or worse or more enlightened than another; the issue is one of quality. For example, the color blue is different from orange but neither one is better or worse; they are merely different. This lack of understanding is apparent in the following quote from Jung, "There are still Negroes today whose 'thoughts' are localized principally in the belly, and Pueblo Indians 'think' with their hearts—'only madmen think with their heads,' they say. On this level of consciousness is essentially passion and the experience of oneness" (1971, p. 544). The value judgments on both sides of this discussion are obvious and only serve to separate the worlds.

The idea of worldviews and systems of conceptualizing the world was not foreign to Jung; he did address these ideas in his Nietzsche lectures:

> With the point of view of that time, then, Nietzsche assumes that those other worlds have been only the imagination of suffering people, while the point is just that suffering people have such imaginations, and that they are as real as they can be. You see, there are plenty of situations in life where your imagination about it is far more important than the situation in itself. Usually the world is what you imagine it to be, and we don't know to what degree that is true; it might be that our world would be quite different if we had a different imagination about it. I am certain for instance, that the primitives live in an entirely different world from ours; we assume that it is the same, but that is by no means true. They have different impressions, different imaginations about it; it functions in an entirely different way. Only a short time ago, any educated Chinaman—not a modern Chinaman—was quite convinced that magic worked, and he was equally convinced that it did not work with a European because a European is not built that way. It does not grip him anywhere; he is not accessible to it. But with them it really does work; it is not mere imagination, because they live in a world and they have a psychology where such

things are possible. We are not accessible-apparently—but I have my doubts about that. (1988, p. 341)

It is apparent from this discussion that Jung understood that there are differences in worldviews. Jung's understanding is made explicit in his statement that the "European is not built that way." Even though there are differences, Jung believed that it was possible to bridge these views: "We are not accessible—apparently—but I have my doubts about that."

Whenever one is engaged in therapist-centered therapy it becomes imperative that the therapist understands not only his/her typological process but that of the patient as well. The therapist should know if his/her dominant attitude is introverted, extroverted, or any combination of attitudes. When the therapist knows his/her own typology, this allows the therapist to be centered regardless of the typology of the patient. What happens when the patient is a traditional Native American who has to fit into Jung's typological scheme? Is it possible that the scheme postulated by Jung may not fit and may need modification? Answers to these questions must come from within the worldview that is best qualified to deal with the issue—that is, from a Native American standpoint. Otherwise, we are again falling into the psychologically colonialistic trap into which most of Western psychology has plummeted.

In order to begin to understand how this different way of conceptualizing typology occurs, it is necessary recall the discussion of Native American worldviews presented earlier. The notion that everything is alive, an integral part of the Native American cosmology, is critical to understanding how Jung's types may have addressed only the Western psyche. For the Westerner, there is a distinct separation between psyche and world, very much in the manner in which Descartes described in his decree of *cogito ergo sum*, Descartes made explicit a process that was undergoing assimilation in the Western psyche; the psychology described by Descartes was one which Jung defined as an extroverted/thinking/sensation attitude.

The extroverted / thinking / sensation attitude clearly describes the separation between subject and object in the Western psyche. The separation of the psyche was also an integral part of how Jung himself saw the world. It is only reasonable to postulate that most of his constructs should be read with this in mind; the reader should realize that Jung's interpretation of psyche was indeed a Western one. The fact that Jung's thinking was of Western origins is not to say that Jung did not offer significant insights into other worldviews; his greatest contribution is perhaps this method of approach to the psyche which allows for our reinterpretation of his theoretical constructs.

Within the Native American view, psyche is an integral part of the actual life that holds the Earth itself as an organism. This cosmology allows for complete harmony with those Earth forces or spirits giving the "being in the world" of the personal and collective group a completely different aspect. That way of being in the world is not accurately captured by the participation mystique notion that has been promoted by anthropology. Anthropological definitions are merely observations from the point of reference of a Western cosmology and may only serve to describe events of this nature to the Western mind.

The notion of typology can be said to have existed in the cosmology of Native American people in pre-Colombian times. For most Native American people the idea of praying to the six cardinal directions was an integral part of day-to-day life, although the six cardinal points had a different flavor than did Jung's six cardinal types. For Native American people there is a spiritual presence at each of these directions which gives a specific type of wisdom, teaching, and relationship to the world. Being at the center of and in balance with all of the directions is reflected in Jung's statement that there is no inferior function at the center. Joseph Campbell describes the notion as follows: "Four symbolical colors, representing the points of the compass, play a prominent role in Navaho iconography and cult. They are white, blue, yellow, and black, signifying, respectfully, east, south, west, and north. These correspond to the red, white, green, and black on the hat of the African trickster divinity Edshu for the House of the Father, like the Father himself, symbolizes the Center" (1973, p. 132).

Figure 2 describes a different typological paradigm. The reader has noticed there are two types on the left hand side of the diagram. The Earth spirit gives the person an instant reality or sensation, which allows for the emergence of what the Westerner knows as intuition. According to a Native American way of interpretation, the individual is actually in synchronization with Earth forces that already have the awareness of all things. The individual has merely placed him/herself in a place in which s/he can be permeated by that awareness, i.e., within the *axis mundi*. Therefore, the individual is sensing and intuiting in the Western sense, but within the experience there is harmony between the Earth spirit and the individual's spirits—which is ultimately part of the spirit of all things. We are part of all creations whether seen or unseen (perceived or not perceived). When we are in accord with those forces there is a keen awareness of all of those forces.

The notion of the center containing the balance—where the creator enacts all things—is well delineated by Gene Thin Elk (1990). In his teaching discussions, Thin Elk describes the four directions as well as the fifth and sixth cardinal points, Heaven and Earth. At the center of the six points is what he terms the "seventh sacred direction," which is synonymous with Wakan Tanka (Creator). The interesting idea here is that the center is within all things.

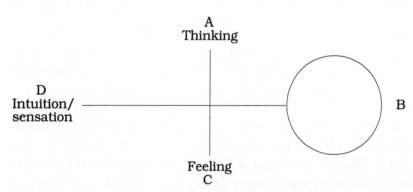

Figure 2. The difference is in that intuition/sensation fall on one side of the figure thus leaving "hole" one the other side (Duran 1990, p. 54).

The client usually comes for treatment because s/he is out of balance. In the process of the therapeutic encounter the client should be able to come to the center of themselves or to find the seventh sacred direction within. The therapist should, in the span of the therapeutic encounter, at least be able to be in touch with his/her own center, otherwise the therapist's imbalance will only throw the client even further out of balance. When the therapist is operating from the center the treatment process is one of therapist-centered therapy; the old notion of the patient being responsible for the balance does not hold in this system, at least initially. As the client becomes able to operate from his/her own seventh sacred direction, the therapist, by removing him/herself from the client's way, allows the client the freedom to discover his/her own mythological and cosmological reality. By centering the therapy the client is empowered into balance. The restoration of balance allows the client to regain his/her relationship with the center of all things. The center of all things is Wakan or sacred, and it is the relationship of the client's center that is restored back with Wakan. The principle of using medicines in a traditional way also encompasses the notion of restoring the center. According to Thin Elk, since the herb or plant used in the healing remains at the center, the medicine empowers the client to recover his/her own center.

Jung was not a total stranger to the idea of Earth forces interacting within the psyche as a harmonious relationship with the Earth. Evidence of Jung's awareness is clear in the Zarathustra seminars (lecture 3, 1988) as Jung states:

> You probably noticed that peculiar expression, the "four square" body. the body is of course very much the earth, and "it speaketh of the meaning of the earth" means that inasmuch as the body has produced consciousness, it produces the meaning of the earth. If you could give consciousness or a creative mind to a book for instance, or to any kind of object, it would speak its contents; give consciousness to wood and it speaks the meaning of wood; give it to stone and it speaks the meaning of stone. . . . This shows that if one remains persistent in the hidden, unspoken purpose, then

the very nature of the earth, the hidden lines in the earth will lead you. (p. 356)

Even though there appears to be more than just an intuitive awareness of Earth harmony, Jung does not weave this notion into the basic development of the types discussion in his collected works. The fact that there is some awareness of this Earth context, however, is cause for optimism, since the bridge between the cosmologies may not be as great of an obstacle as some may think.

In our diagram of the integrated Native American typological construct, the hole on the right-hand side of the quadrant is in need of explanation. It is through this hole or "emptiness" that it is possible to walk into the transcendent with awareness and knowledge which is given by the spirits of all creation. This function takes us out of the realm of sensation or intuition and places us in a place that is sacred. Within the Western worldview this is the place of sensation. It is our view that most sensation or reality testing which relies on perception has been fundamental to the scientific attitude as developed in the West. Scientism is what has removed the Western psyche from the ability to have that close relationship with creation. Sensation or perception used in the constructing of a quantifiable world can make sense only in the logical positivistic paradigm. In order to remove the door to allow for transcendental experiences to be valid, the Western psyche must deal with its subject-object split. A sure way of opening the door is through the complete loss of reality testing of the sensation function as in the case of psychosis.

The balance of the types in Native American cosmology can be portrayed by the idea of the seventh sacred direction. The center is where the spatiotemporal reality becomes united with the transcendental and becomes the *axis mundi* within our realm of existence. As most traditional teachers agree, it is equally as out of balance to be on the sacred side of reality as it is to simply live life in a totally profane manner. The center allows for the relationship of humans to the sacred while still maintaining a relationship with the Earth and all creations in a balanced approach to life.

Jung also reports having an experience of "oneness" with the world during his life. There was a day when Jung was sitting on a rock, but suddenly he was not sure if he was the rock or the observer (1965, p. 20). This experience can be explained by a Western cosmology or a Native American one. The important thing here is that there was an experience. Whatever the thinking and feeling functions decide to do with it in terms of explanation and value are heavily loaded with the evolution of the world cosmologies which make up those functions. The reader may argue that some of these functions need to occur within the thinking function, but thinking is usually derived from the cosmology and experiences of the culture that gives the thinking its peculiar cultural flavor.

In E.D.'s previous work *Archetypal Consultation*, he fell into the error of interpreting the type problem from the Western worldview. One explanation for this is that when a Native American person is in the process of writing a dissertation in a Western graduate school there are certain things which are not acceptable; one of those things is thinking in a different cultural context. Therefore, E.D. had to stretch the Jungian perspective as far as it would go, and in retrospect that stretching was not accurate in light of the present discussion. In this section of theoretical formulation we are presenting ideas that E.D. was not able to present due to the limitations of graduate education in a Euro-American context.

An error that E.D. made in the theorizing discussion of this earlier work was the statement that the Native American psyche was differentiated in a different direction than the Western psyche. The Western psyche found itself at point A of the diagram in figure 2, while the Native American psyche was more *phrenes* (feeling) and conceptualizing was still being done in a more prephilosophical fashion. In this, the assumption was made that the Native American psyche had to move more toward point A if the Native American psyche was to survive in the colonialistic society. In that discussion E.D. also alluded to the fact that in working with Western people, the therapy should focus on moving them out of A toward the phrenes (feeling) area of the diagram designated B. The discussion of moving toward A or B was predicated on the fact that E.D. had incorporated a content and linear way of describing the psyche, since he was trapped in a situation which demanded Western explanations.

A clear example of Jung being trapped by his own cosmology is demonstrated in a conversation he had with Mountain Lake. Jung tells us:

> If we explain our scientific views to the intelligent native he will accuse us of ludicrous superstitiousness and a disgraceful want of logic, for he believes that the world is lighted by the sun and not the human eye. My friend Mountain Lake, a Pueblo chief, once called me sharply to account because I had made insinuating use of the Augustinian argument; "Not this sun is our lord, but he who made the sun." Pointing to the sun he cried indignantly: "He who goes there is our father. You can see him. From him comes all light, all life—there is nothing that he has not made." He became greatly excited, struggled for words, and finally cried out: "even a man in the mountains who goes alone, cannot make fire without him." (1964, p. 68)

The differences in worldviews are palpable in this passage in that Jung was trapped by his intellect and Mountain Lake realized that all energy comes from the sun. The fact that Mountain Lake realized that not even fire was possible without the sun is clearly something to which Jung should have listened, at least symbolically. As we all know, fire symbolizes spirit and libido, without which we do not exist regardless of worldview. It is the fundamental way of experiencing the world that is at issue here, and the Western therapist should avoid the trap of thinking that his/her thinking is quantitatively and/or qualitatively superior.

The discussion so far makes perfect sense to most people who are schooled in Jungian psychology, since it falls into the logical positivistic paradigm. The most important facts that have not been clarified are some of the type issues discussed above, and the fact that there is a completely different psychology working in the Native American psyche. Critical notions when dealing with thinking versus feeling in respect to cosmology are not who has a certain inferior function or superior function and to which linear direction the type is to differentiate; the essence of the discussion should focus on the manner of approach to "being in the world" when it comes to working with any of the types.

When dealing with thinking and feeling in a Native American context, we should leave value definitions aside and try to find some root metaphors that guide the psychological makeup of the people. What is critical in thinking and feeling is that these functions emerge from the Earth knowledge and intuition. It is well known that the basic underlying principle of Native American typological functions is Earth or the feminine. History abounds with examples of how Western culture has been dominated by a patriarchal worldview and how the feminine has been all but in exile from the Western psyche. On the other hand, the beginning student of Native American cosmology knows that most tribal groups in the Wew World were and are matriarchal. Therefore, we have a basic difference in cosmology: Western cosmology is masculine and Native American cosmology is more in alignment with the feminine.

A thinking function that has its root metaphors in masculine psychology is going to be diametrically opposed to a thinking function that is feminine. When we bring the other two cardinal points into the picture (extroversion and introversion), we have a vast number of permutations of a type completely different from those theorized by Jung. For instance, a Native American may be a thinking/sensation/extroverted type, but his/her psychology will be fundamentally different than that of a Western person of similar typological structure because of the basic difference in worldview. Jung did a very fine job conceptualizing types for the Westerner, and his notions of "anima" and "animus" alluded to the basic differences in the description of types. Jung's own psyche, though, was a product of Western evolution and his theoretical ideas, though useful to non-Western people, are in need of further development if the ideas are to be practical for non-Westerners. Even though Jung included the anima-animus notion in his theory, there is still a distinct disconnectedness from the Earth or the great mother because the Earth has been severed from the Western psyche.

An issue that is usually denied in most psychological literature is the one dealing with the conquest of Native American people. Taking some of the notions mentioned thus far in this theoretical formulation, it is no mystery as to what happened. The Western masculine cosmology literally raped the New World. The rape occurred at all levels of the Native American experience; rape was done to the Earth as well at to the people who were in close harmony with the Earth spirits. The Western way of being in the world has been systematically forced on Native American people in such brutal and genocidal proportions that there has been a wound severing their connectedness with the Earth.

In this new way of formulating typology, when there is a severing at the sensation/intuition of figure 2, something must complement this. What has happened is that the hole no longer serves the transcendent function in the prescribed traditional manner. The hole previously provided a path whereby the individual and community had a shamanic window or ability to directly commune with the spirits. Now the hole function has been left vacant and it appears that a different type of spirit has occupied the function—the hole function has been filled by alcohol spirits, which provide an unhealthy relationship with the sacred. The person who is trapped in the delusional worship of the alcohol spirits may sever his/her relationship with the six cardinal points and be completely out of balance. Where we once used to go in complete confidence and trust has now turned into darkness and despair. The filling in of the hole and its manifestations receive in-depth discussion part 2. Suffice it to say that in order to recapture the relationship with the transcendent, Native Americans must find the true Earth spirits once again and give the spirits in the bottle back to their rightful owners.

Bear in mind that these two cosmologies are simply different and that value judgments should be suspended. After all, the cosmologies—whether they are Western or Native American—have a similar source, and we really do not have the overall picture as to where the evolution of the collective psyche is moving. It is apparent that through discussions and integration of thinking, it will be possible for people from different cosmologies to have an experiential realization of a different cosmology, which might help to bring the worlds closer.

In doing interventions with Native American people, it is important that the practitioner assimilate some of the notions expressed in this chapter because these are some of the premises that have heretofore been the underlying factors impeding the delivery of relevant treatment to Native American populations. In our experience, keeping Native American people in treatment as long as necessary has not been a problem. This is remarkable since the literature indicates that minority clients usually do not stay in treatment for more than three sessions (Sue and Zane 1987, p. 37).

Part 2

Clinical Praxis

Faith without works is dead.

—St. Paul

The preceding discussion was offered in order to acquaint the serious student, social scientist, or practitioner with some realizations that are important before embarking on the process of working clinically with Native American patients or clients. Reading this book is not sufficient for the therapist to begin to dispense therapist-centered therapy to clients. This discussion merely provides a basic understanding that is useful to the therapist as s/he works under the guidance of someone who is experienced in working within the different worldviews.

We have been able to train several students in the past few years to do some of the work described so far; for the most part, this has been very painful for the student. During the very early stages of the training, most students become frustrated because it seems that all of the interventions that they have used successfully in the past no longer show any effectiveness. These students find themselves in an experience in which they start to doubt their own reality and value system. This makes them vulnerable to experiences and realizations that are completely foreign to them. Most students find themselves wanting to quit the internship early since the fantasy of working with Native Americans is not the romantic process of enlightening the savages some would like to think. Instead, their own psychological process plunges them deep into a world of unknown forces which threaten the very existence of their ego reality.

In the next chapters we delineate some basic therapeutic interventions that have been useful in our work. These interventions must not be used without proper supervision by someone who is knowledgeable of some of the traditional cosmologies. Jung is wise in his cautioning of therapists: "For this reason to dabble in psychotherapy is to play with fire, against which amateurs should be stringently cautioned. It is particularly dangerous when the mythological layer of psyche is uncovered, for these contents have a fearful fascination to the patient which explains the tremendous influence mythological ideas have had on mankind" (1954, p. 15). The student should heed this caution since it is especially risky when s/he is exposed to a psyche that is not congruent with his/her own. The seduction of or curiosity about working with Native Americans can lead to confusion and pathological symptoms if the student is not well grounded in his/her own tradition. In order to ground students, we always ask them to find their own tribe and to gain understanding of the traditional beliefs of their ancestors.

In E.D.'s previous work, *Archetypal Consultation,* the point of not revealing case material was discussed. We have since discovered that clinical material may perhaps be of help to therapists who work with Native American people, and thus should not remain sealed. One of the greatest reasons for this is that at this time we have gained enough distance from the material both psychologically and geographically. We have worked in many settings in the past decade, thus safeguarding the confidentiality of these patients. Also, we can be more objective with the case material at this time, especially since we are not presently treating those patients.

Some of the strategies that we have presented have had strange reactions from journal reviewers—one even remarked, "this scares me" (Review letter from Psych. Reports, 1991). Perhaps this fright was not from the material itself as much as from his lack of understanding and inability to step out of his own cosmological paradigm.

Toward Trauma Mastery and the Mending of the Hoop

The current Native American situation has been and is very painful to the brothers and sisters involved in the suffering, but there are several possible solutions. One can take the existential approach and simply be satisfied in finding ultimate meaning in the suffering. The authors, however, believe that there can be meaning in the suffering and that greater meaning will emerge in the healing of the wounds that have afflicted our people for centuries. As in any other type of therapy or healing, there first needs to be awareness of the trauma before any long-term healing can occur. Ideally we should be able to bring the perpetrator into the therapeutic encounter, thus beginning his healing as well; at this time the perpetrators are still in denial of the genocide of unparalleled proportions of which they are guilty. With or without the perpetrator, healing can occur; the rest of this section examines the healing that is possible for the Native American community.

In discussing any type of therapeutic intervention with Native Americans, it becomes critical to discuss cross-cultural issues from a perspective that is usually not found in most therapeutic literature. The simple reason for the failure of most therapies performed on Native American populations is that most of the therapies are Western-based and irrelevant for Native Americans. According to Duran (1990), many Western therapies are merely methods of colonizing the lifeworld of the Native American client. The end result of many Western therapies is the ongoing cultural hegemony of the client seeking help. Even though the efficacy of the therapeutic arena seems doubtful when the analysis places it in a colonialistic paradigm, there are some integrated approaches that have been found to be effective (Duran 1990).

Most literature on minorities in therapy indicates that people of color drop out of treatment before their third visit, and it has been proposed that exposure to orthodox Western psychotherapy is harmful to ethnic minorities (LaFromboise and Rowe 1983; Lefley and Pedersen 1986). Since Western therapies appear to be ineffective and even harmful for non-Westerners, must the problems go untreated or unattended? Fortunately, some success has been demonstrated in working with Native American populations in the recent past. Duran has developed rural and urban models of intervention for Native American populations. In both of these models the evaluation of the project demonstrated effectiveness through several measures. The simplest measure of success was that of return visits. The other measure of success was provided by the community through qualitative evaluation of the effectiveness of the project (Duran 1984, 1990).

The models of treatment that are the most effective are those in which traditional Native American thinking and practice are utilized in conjunction with Western practice. In order to accomplish this integration, the therapist must understand and validate traditional Native American cosmology. In essence, the therapist cannot simply learn to apply cross-cultural techniques in the hope that these will help the client. The therapist must believe and practice these beliefs in his/her personal life if the intervention is to benefit the client. There is nothing more offensive to a Native American client than a therapist who is pretending to understand and provide therapy within a traditional perspective if that therapist is merely mimicking a value system through the production of therapeutic techniques.

The models developed by Duran were successful because of their validation of traditional values. For instance, the San Francisco Bay Area urban model started with neither services nor clients being served for mental health problems; within a period of two years there were over one hundred clients being served every month. The only limitation to the amount of clients served was a fiscal one, and once more services were provided the program begin to serve over two hundred clients per month. Of the clients served over a two-year period, many of them returned for ongoing therapy twenty times, which is almost seven times the return rate in orthodox programs. In addition, over several years it was noted that the range of diagnostic categories were as varied as they are for any group. Interestingly enough, a majority of the clients (at least 75 percent) also exhibited symptoms that qualified for the diagnosis of PTSD.

The component that is critical to this model is the traditional one. It is not enough that the program have a traditional component; the program must have traditional Native American psychology as its core metaphor. There are some problems that must be bridged in doing so because there are so many distinct tribal groups and the compilation of a generic Native American philosophy is ludicrous. This model attempts to serve people of various tribes from a perspective of respect to the particular tribe and individual. The therapy focuses on implementing the client's belief system and is facilitated through dream interpretation. If there is one central tradition among a majority of tribes, it is the tradition of the dream being a core spiritual and psychological reality. The treatment models developed by Duran (1984, 1989) have demonstrated that a key element in working with Native American people from many tribes is the interpretation of dreams in a traditional context.

In addition to serving the client from a perspective of respect and dream interpretation, the program has also incorporated traditional counselors and traditional medicine people as a core component of the project. Again, the emphasis is on core versus periphery. Many programs that incorporate traditional approaches usually have the traditional component serve as a complement to the Western service delivery model. This practice is disrespectful and dooms the program to failure. For instance, if the traditional provider does not have the same professional status as does the Western professional provider, the program is merely continuing the hegemonic practice that has been part of the policy of white medicine for many years.

At the Family and Child Guidance Clinic that is a part of the Urban Native American Health Board in the San Francisco/Oakland area, such a model has been incorporated with great success. The program has on staff a traditional Western-trained counselor as well as having funding available to have medicine people occasionally visit from out of state. The traditional program has integrated the sweat lodge ceremony as part of its treatment and prevention strategy. Psychologists in conjunction with the traditional providers participate in the diagnosis as well as treatment plan of the client. The consulting medicine people not only see clients but also are part of the clinical case conference that is designed to provide the best treatment strategy for the individual.

A typical protocol for a client is as follows:

1. Client is referred to either the traditional counselor or psychologist for intervention. The referral is usually made from various community social agencies or from other traditional providers.

2. The traditional counselor or psychologist makes an assessment of the client and immediately has a conference with the other providers. The case is also taken to the staff conference at which time all counselors, social workers, and providers plan a course of treatment for the client.

3. The client then receives psychotherapy as well as participates in traditional ceremonies as appropriate. If the client needs help from a medicine person, then s/he is referred to a medicine person from his/her traditional belief system or told when the consulting medicine person will be spending time at the clinic. The therapy that the client receives is designed to help the client understand the process itself. Many Native American clients have been so acculturated that many times the focus of the therapy is merely to reconnect them to a traditional system of belief and make sense of their lifeworld from a traditional perspective. Caution should be taken by the reader so that there will not be a confusion of traditional approaches and reconnection with the romanticizing of tradition that is so popular these days. The client must be helped to understand and to work at coping in the actual lifeworld that is around them, and for the most part the client must be able to adjust and work in a white environment as well as still maintain a sense of identity. This is difficult if not impossible for the therapist who has not had to do so in his/her own life.

At times, therapy takes place outside of an agency office setting and within a traditional sweat lodge. The psychologist must work closely with traditional colleagues in order to best facilitate the therapeutic intervention. Many Western-trained providers become nervous at what appears to be lack of therapeutic boundaries. This fear only materializes if the Western provider is not aware of the traditional healing boundaries, which are in fact more stringent than Western ethics.

4. The client is evaluated and recommendations are made for ongoing therapy or participation in traditional ceremonies as appropriate. Unlike Western psychotherapy, the traditional cosmology of treatment does not compartmentalize the personality. There is no termination from Tradition as there is from Western psychotherapy. The psychologist working in such a clinic must understand that Western therapeutic boundaries may be inappropriate at times and the client may continue to ask for help at ceremonial places even after the official therapy has terminated. For example, if therapy is terminated and the psychologist is participating in a sweat lodge ceremony that week, the client may come to the psychologist and exchange some small talk that will also involve some issues that were part of the therapy. If the psychologist holds to rigid Western boundaries and insists that the person make an appointment, then the client may be offended and feel belittled. This also confuses the client because this event is taking place at a ceremony at which people are not discouraged from talking about issues.

When clients present themselves with a domestic violence situation, the therapy must take into account the historical overview as outlined earlier. There is no way that the client can begin to deal with the issues of violence in the family without understanding the dynamics of the historical violence perpetrated on Native American people by the European colonization process. Some therapists react with guilt, which is usually manifested in their pointing out that this colonization happened a long time ago and we must help the client in the here and now. If the therapist understands the intergenerational effects of PTSD, the therapist will obviously not make such hegemonic observations. If the client is to own his/her part of the therapeutic dynamic, then it is imperative that the therapist (if s/he is of are Western descent) own his/her part in the historical dynamic. Therapist refusal to own his/her history results in a dishonest exchange which merely facilitates shutdown by the clients, who consequently probably drop out of treatment.

Once the client understands that much of the pathology affecting his/her family system is indeed systemic, the client can then rid him/herself of some of the guilt that s/he is carrying over his/her violent acts against his/her community. Since guilt is a useless emotion and is only conducive to more pathology, it is critical to exorcise it from the therapy as soon as possible. The systemic approach also allows the client to rejoin the human family and see an opportunity for healing. This opportunity for healing can then be paved through the traditional healing and education process. We cannot sufficiently emphasize that by the client getting in touch with his/her Native American identity the therapy is accomplishing a twofold task:

1. The client is improving his/her self-esteem and sense of identity, which correlate with healthy functioning.

2. Through becoming aware of historical factors the process will be facilitated whereby the client is able to rid him/herself of the internalized oppressor. The exorcising of the internalized oppressor is one of the biggest accomplishments that the client can make in the therapy process. Ridding of the oppressor can only be effected through the implementation of the integrated model of therapy. If there is no integrated model of treatment then the client is once more hearing that only white models are valid, thus facilitating a deeper internalization of the oppressor. It is quite obvious that at this point the therapy is becoming a coconspirator in the family violence rather than acting in its healing.

5

The Spirit of Alcohol

My grandmother thought of alcohol as a bad spirit. She treated it like it was a spirit. She talked to it like it was a person standing close to her. She said she didn't take alcohol and throw it aside angrily. She told the alcohol to go away from her. She said she put it in a bag and tied it up. She put it aside and said it would be there all the time. She didn't get angry at it. She didn't get down on it. She put it aside without anger in a Native American way. That way it wouldn't come back on her. She didn't want it to hurt her or come back to her bad side. Some people try to quit and they get down on the alcohol. In a Native American way, that's angrily pushing it aside. The alcohol retaliates and goes back to the person. It comes back to the person. It comes back to the bad side and doubles its strength. This makes a person take a hard fall. The important thing is the way you let go of a bad spirit, so it does not come back on you. When I quit drinking, I used that as an example. I put it aside and don't bother it. That way it won't come back to your bad side and make you worse.

—Francis Auld, interview with Michael Raymond, 1980

Our treatment of the issue of alcoholism does not follow an orthodox method in a clinical or theoretical paradigm. The first part of this chapter deals with existing literature on the subject of alcoholism among Native Americans from a Western academic perspective. The authors then present ideas that were first presented in the 1700s and have recently been substantiated by empirical study. The authors then discuss contemporary traditional and clinical interventions that utilize the notions delineated in the first part of the book. By structuring the chapter in this fashion the authors hope that the reader will realize that solutions to the problem of alcohol have been offered by the traditional community for centuries. Academia's more recent interest in the problem has offered few if any new solutions or explanations for the problem.

Alcohol-Related Mortality

In 1984 Native Americans died due to alcoholism, alcohol psychosis, and cirrhosis of the liver at a rate of 30 per 100,000. Although this rate is nearly half the 1969 rate of 56.6 per 100,000, it is still 4.8 times the 1984 all races rate of 6.2 deaths per 100,000 population (Indian Health Service 1987). In addition to deaths due directly to diseases related to alcoholism, alcohol is considered a large contributing factor in suicides, homicides, other intentional and unintentional injuries, and mental health problems (Berlin 1985; Conrad and Kahn 1974; Havighurst 1971; Long 1986; May 1982, 1986; Resnick 1971; Shore et al. 1973; Spaulding 1986). Homicide and diabetes death rates, which are much higher for Native Americans than for all races combined, have been linked to alcohol use and abuse among Native American populations.

The myth of the drunken Native American has persisted in this country from colonial times to the present. Given the misconception that Native Americans cannot hold their liquor and the very real alcohol-related public health problems for Native Americans, we might assume that research and programs addressing these problems would abound. However, although some anthropological research has been conducted in this century, only since the 1970s has the problem been addressed seriously by the Indian Health Service (IHS) and other health care providers.

Most of the academic literature on the prevalence of alcoholism in the Native American community and on Native American treatment programs has focused on the sociocultural etiologies of use and barriers to recovery, psychopathology, personality characteristics, treatment outcomes, and on peyote as a treatment alternative. Articles focusing on sociocultural etiologies almost universally include poverty, poor housing, relative ill-health, academic failures, cultural conflict with the majority society, and racism as some of the main predisposing factors for Native American alcoholism (Barnes and Welte 1986; Beauvais and LaBoueff 1985; Beauvais, Oetting, and Edwards 1985; Fisher 1984; ; Jilek-Aäll 1978; Murphy and DeBlassie 1984). Most of these articles lead the reader to believe that poverty, academic failure, and cultural conflict are Native American problems that exist in an acontextual fashion. These articles usually do not make mention that these problems are a direct result of the policies of the U.S. government toward Native American people.

Some researchers have narrowed the problem further by citing laissez-faire child-rearing practices, parental and community attitudes about drug use, and conflicts between cultural ideas and behavioral realities as factors contributing to the high prevalence of substance abuse among Native American adolescents (Weibel-Orlando 1984). It is amazing that literature of this type is accepted without any critical analysis of what the author means by laissez-faire child-rearing practices. The erroneous assumption to which this research can lead is that Native American people do not care about their children and therefore it is the lack of caring that leads to alcoholism and drug abuse. Again, no mention of historical factors is made and the culpability is placed on the culture itself.

Tribal affiliation and age were found to influence drinking styles and the attitudes toward alcohol in one study of an urban Native American population (Weisner, Weibel-Orlando, and Long 1984). In this study, American cultural values of individualism and individual choice are at odds with the traditional Native American values of consensus and community and are discussed as a barrier to Native American recovery within a majority culture framework (Katz 1979; Yellowthunder 1981). Indeed, Katz (1979) sees the pull between the two cultures as inevitably unreconcilable.

Psychopathology within the population is often cited as a determining factor in Native American substance abuse. Anxiety, depression, psychological distortion, and maladjustment are seen as prevalent in urban Native American communities (Borunda and Shore 1978; Graves 1973), whereas depression, mania, neurosis, and schizophrenia are common diagnoses for reservation-based Native Americans (Berlin 1985; Harvey, Gazay, and Samuels 1976; Pelz 1981; Shen 1986; Shore et al. 1973; Westermeyer and Neider 1984a, 1984b). Mental health problems were found to be exacerbated for Native Americans in urban settings because of a lack of both social support and accessible treatment for mental disorders (Barter and Barter 1974). Native Americans in alcoholic treatment programs were found to be highly pathological, reflected in elevated scores on scales for cynicism, disorganized thinking, hypochondriasis, ideas of persecution, repression, self-depreciation, and somatic complaints when compared to scores for white inpatients (Hoffman and Jackson 1973). These scores should be interpreted carefully since most of the psychological instruments used on Native American people have not been normed for a Native American population. Test scores are biased against Native American people and culture in that many phenomena that are normal within Native American life are deemed pathological by test instruments such as the Minnesota Multiphasic Personality Inventory (MMPI). Alaskan native populations are thought to be suffering from frequent paranoid personality disorders, which have been positively correlated with westernization and increases in non-native population size (Foulks and Katz 1973). The fact that the Alaskan native population was and is actually being oppressed and persecuted apparently never crossed the mind of the researcher when the diagnosis of paranoid personality was applied. In our view, the fact that Native American people sometimes score as paranoid may reflect good reality testing rather than pathological disorders.

Personality characteristics of Native American alcoholics in treatment are a popular research topic, although most research done on Native Americans is performed by non-Native American researchers and agencies. Results from MMPI evaluations have determined that this population is "fairly seriously disturbed" when compared to white alcoholic populations (Edwards and Edwards 1984; Kline et al. 1973; Shen, Sanchez, and Huang 1984), as well as finding the tendency for both female and male Native American alcoholics to exhibit a high level of "toughmindedness" (Gade and Hurlburt 1985; Hurlburt, Gade, and Fuqua 1984). This high level of toughmindedness can also be interpreted as a survival mechanism in the face of having to live in a society in which Native Americans are systematically denied the opportunity to live a life that is meaningful within their cultural context.

Alcoholism treatment outcome evaluations for Native American patients, although contradictory, indicate a very low level of success. One study on the effects of treatment for Native American adolescents in a mixed race facility cited a more positive outcome for whites (Query 1985), while another study for Native American adults cited a 95 percent recidivism rate (Kivalahan et al. 1985). It has been found that female Native American alcoholics are unlikely to deteriorate and still survive (Westermeyer and Neider 1984). One ten-year alcohol treatment follow-up study (Westermeyer and Peak 1983) found 16 percent of subjects recovered and another 22 percent dead from alcohol-related causes. One study cited a 44 percent "improvement rate" while warning against erroneous judgment of Native American drinking status by non-Native American health workers (Wilson and Shore 1975). Most of the success rates in most IHS programs with which we have worked do not have well-defined criteria for success; therefore, when reading successful outcomes it is difficult to ascertain if the success is short-term or long-term. The number of deaths due to alcoholism are indicative that the successes are not long-term.

Peyote has received considerable attention as a useful ethnopharmacologic agent in alcohol dependency treatment (Blum, Futterman, and Pascarosa 1977). This approach is considered an appropriate treatment alternative because of its use in the Native American Church and its properties that enhance "suggestibility" (Albaugh and Anderson 1974). Other research cites the possible "lasting and permanent effect . . . (by) promoting self-actualization and spiritual consciousness" which is missing from orthodox Western approaches (Pascarosa and Futterman 1976). None of the authors dealing with the issue of peyote give any validity to peyote as "medicine" within the Native American worldview. Is it possible that peyote is exactly what Native American people say it is? Native Americans believe that peyote helps attain insight through visions, which enhance the healing process and diminish the need for alcohol. This makes sense when seen from the theoretical perspective presented in chapter 4 (i.e., peyote may be the vehicle that fills the void and helps to restore balance in the psyche).

Current prevalence studies have been concentrated on finding the levels of substance use among Native American adolescent populations. One study of over 10,000 Native American youth found a slight decrease in alcohol and drug use after 1981 for all substances except marijuana. Even with this promising turn of events, more than 53 percent of Native American adolescents surveyed were "at risk" for serious drug involvement (Beauvais, Oetting, and Edwards 1985). When this is seen in light of the devastation of fetal alcohol syndrome, which is affecting many Native American youth and which will continue for generations, the picture becomes grim and the people researching psychopathology among Native American people should realize that there may be reason for depression and anxiety.

Another popular research topic within the context of Native American alcoholism is the validation and/or use of psychological testing instruments. Instruments created and validated for the dominant culture such as the Jackson Differential Personality Inventory (Hoffman and Jackson 1973), the Holtzman Inkblot Inventory (Query and Query 1972), the Wechsler Intelligence Scale for Children-Revised [WISC-R] (McShane and Plas 1984), the Eysenck Personality Questionnaire (Hurlburt, Gade, and Fuqua 1982), the ever-popular MMPI (Page and Bozlee 1982), and the Ego Strength Scale (Peniston 1978) are used to provide analysis of individual Native Americans' drinking in order to categorize deviance. The deviance that these tests are measuring is based on the standard of normality in the dominant white population.

The use of modern Western psychology continues to be the main method of trying to understand the problems within Native American country. The frustrating issue in all of these methods is that these researchers are using tools from the very cultural context that has been oppressing Native Americans. Have any of these researchers heard of experimenter bias and transference—and how these have a fundamental effect on most human interactions?

In addition to research on the treatment and etiology of dysfunctional Native American drinking, health and social science professionals have attempted to establish a relationship between drinking and another serious health problem facing Native Americans—suicide (more on this issue chap. 7). Research into the relationship between alcohol and other public health issues such as homicide and injuries has not been extensively undertaken. Although many researchers assume a link (Beauvais, Oetting, and Edwards 1985; Berlin 1985; May 1986), only a few studies investigating violence and other intentional and unintentional injuries have reached the academic journals. One study investigating the high postnatal death rates for Native Americans (twice the U.S. white rate) found that unsafe living conditions causing preventable accidents accounted for part of this high rate of death for infants under one year of age (Honigfeld and Kaplan 1987). Other examinations of alcohol-related violence and injuries in Native American communities have been undertaken in Canada.

Most alcohol and drug abuse prevention programs currently operating in Native American country have been initiated by IHS personnel and tribal community members. Lack of funding, academic publishing interests, and expertise prove to be barriers to extensive evaluation and knowledge of such projects. As one study has indicated, however, some prevention is better than no prevention and comparisons of projects with widely differing theoretical bases have resulted in no significant variation in efficacy between models (Carpenter 1981). How many of the models that were compared were designed and implemented by the community and with Native American traditional values as the premise of the program? Again, we may assume the answer is few, if any.

One intervention that has incorporated experimental design and has found its way into the academic literature has adopted the predominant social influence approach to skills enhancement in order to reduce substance use and abuse within adolescent Native American populations (Schinke, Orlandi, et al. 1988). Other researchers have suggested the use of a social learning approach to combat "nonresponsible drinking behavior and outmoded models of prolonged intoxication" (Bach and Bornstein 1981). Outcomes of this program show significant change in identification as a user and on knowledge of substance abuse with no variation on self-esteem or coping skills.

While the definitive sources of alcohol and drug abuse patterns within the Native American community remain to be established, most experts in the field agree that poverty, discrimination, and a degeneration of Native American culture are contributing factors. Although these circumstances are nearly always emphasized, the focus of research has too often been the individual and his/her maladaptive adjustments to life in the late twentieth century. In essence, this surreptitiously redefines the problem as an individual one with responsibility for prevention or cure placed at the individual level. Although many individual clinicians and researchers as well as Native American community leaders recognize the roots of the problem in a historical relationship of domination and the explicit policy of genocide enacted by the federal government, prevention/intervention strategies do not reflect this understanding.

While we do not mean to suggest that individual psychodynamics are inconsequential to Native American alcoholism, the current findings on the extent of abuse by Native American youth indicate environmental and structural problems on a gross scale. It is the most basic analysis that needs to be performed to realize that the problems must be of sociohistorical proportions. What if the historical context were different? Would the problem be at present proportions? Again, a basic analysis of the simplest type would indicate that the problem would not be so great. Evidence of this is best illustrated by other fourth world peoples—for example, the Aborigines of Australia and other indigenous people of the Western hemisphere—who are having similar difficulties and also share a history of genocide and ethnocide.

The literature concerning treatment and psychopathology is especially revealing. Recent studies have determined that nonwhites are often labeled into harsher diagnostic categories (Lefley 1986), and that culturally bound behavior and social context are essentially disregarded when treatment and prevention plans are established. When culturally bound behavior is regarded, it is viewed as idiosyncratic and given token consideration in a paternalistic framework. This recognition of culture may indicate a dangerous shift of responsibility from the individual to cultural etiologies without consideration of the relationship of individuals in the culture to the economic and political stakeholders in the community. Inappropriate cultural values, beliefs, and behaviors may become the focus of intervention.

What is missing from all but a few of the research projects in Native American country is a recognition that Native American drinking patterns have been historically labeled as deviant whereas white middle-class norms and behaviors have served as the validation criteria. One reason Alcoholics Anonymous (AA) may not be an effective referral for Native Americans suffering from chronic drinking problems is its middle-class orientation and goal of "pointing the road back to our middle-class way of life . . . derived as it is from our dominant Protestant Ethic" (Kurtz 1988). Participation in AA may serve to reinforce feelings of failure and domination, which are theorized by some psychological researchers to be causes of substance abuse (Duran 1990).

Many readers may feel strongly one way or another about the content of the above paragraph. Let us simply say that in no way do we intend to minimize the choice of AA attendance by some Native American people as a way toward achieving a healthier life-style. What we propose is that there are other ways toward achieving this goal within a traditional context. Many times we have worked with Native American people who have been victimized by a treatment approach that is not culturally relevant; when they react to it by expressing negative feelings, they are placed in a double bind by being labeled as "being in denial." AA is a system that places Native American people in a double bind by discounting much of what is culturally valid for Native Americans through the denial-labeling paradigm.

Many clients with whom we have worked as well as other Native American therapists have disclosed to us that many Native American people resent the fact that AA is forced on them in Native American treatment programs. The whole idea of having to refer to the Creator in ways that closely resemble the Christian way is offensive to some of the clients. If the clients are to mention this within the treatment group, they are quickly labeled as being resistant. The worst scenario is that these clients are terminated from treatment if they bring up the issue of not being able to relate to the treatment approach. As termination occurs these clients are made to feel that they are not ready to give up drinking and only when they humble themselves to the place in which they accept the totality of the program will they be able to overcome their alcoholism. This type of treatment has overtones of zealous missionizing that only serves to further increase the gap between the Native American and his/her traditional way of relating with the world. This loss of culture has been shown to be one factor that contributes to unhealthy lifestyle, yet culture is systematically being lost in treatment programs that are not sensitive to the cultural worldview of Native American people. In no way do we minimize the effectiveness of AA or an approach that combines AA with traditional practices if the client chooses this intervention; the lack of choice is what we believe is very destructive in treatment programs.

Prevention strategies aimed at ameliorating Native American alcoholism and substance abuse are inconsistent with the etiology of the problem suggested in the scientific literature. While academicians and health care providers profess to understand the historical, social, and economic factors in alcohol use for Native American populations, most prevention programs aim to fit individuals into middle-class socially prescribed roles. Interventions based on social learning theory define the needs of participants as competency skills to function better in society. What is not recognized is that alcohol use and even suicide may be functional behavioral adaptations within a hostile and hopeless social context.

One area of interest that has received scant research attention is the role of alcohol as a method of social control. Analysis of alcohol as a tool of domination, as theorized by Morgan (1983), Room (1981), and Mosher (1975), is applicable to the development of the problem as it exists today. According to Morgan, a relationship of domination can be established or maintained by alcohol in two interrelated ways, "by increasing or maintaining the power and effective social control of the dominant, and by increasing or maintaining the subordination of the powerless" (1983, p. 410). Alcohol was first introduced into Native American communities by European traders at the time of the invasion of this continent. Traders manipulated Native American hunters into an exchange of goods for alcohol while modeling aggressive and excessive alcohol use (MacAndrews and Edgerton 1969). Following further colonization and settlement, Native American drinking behavior was labeled deviant and a prohibition was established against Native Americans using alcohol. The labeling of Native American drinking behavior as deviant was a method of social control and was one justification for paternalistic policies with the aim of obtaining Native American land. The Native American alcohol prohibition, which lasted until 1953, was used symbolically and instrumentally to promote and maintain a system of domination by denying the use of alcohol to Native American groups. Prohibitions served to isolate Native American group experience from other ethnic communities while reinforcing the values of the majority culture. The beliefs about Native American disinhibition justified the assertions of cultural inferiority and promoted cultural hegemony.

The belief by both the majority culture and Native Americans in the myth of the drunken Native American and the notion that Native American disinhibition produces deviant behavior continues to maintain subjugation. One inherent assumption of current prevention programs is that the only way out of alcohol-related health problems is Native American assimilation and adaptation to the dominant culture. As Mosher states, "current discussions of Native Americans and alcoholism still reflect the dominant white ideas of the general inferiority of Native American culture" (1975, p. 10). The rhetoric of disinhibition and Native Americans may also serve as a face-saving device for Native American communities. Rather than acknowledging the subordinate relationship of tribal councils to federal bureaucracies, tribal leaders may use alcoholism as a viable excuse for victimization.

Alcohol abuse and alcoholism per se, stated as the major problem within Native American communities, serve as an explanation which shifts the focus from more problematic associations. Alcoholism as a disease entity reduces the economic and social problems within Native American communities to medical ones with responsibility for amelioration in the hands of the medical establishment. Alcohol's correlation to suicide, homicide, and injuries is a spurious relationship that preoccupies and distracts us from the multifactorial and structural analysis of the problem.

Native American culture is not a single entity. There is a tremendous amount of variation linguistically, culturally, and religiously among Native American nations in the United States.

Current attempts to incorporate cultural values into treatment and prevention programs usually emphasize the use of traditional ceremonies and healers to enhance feelings of esteem and Native American pride. Although the use of specific cultural artifacts in this context is an important variable in treatment and prevention, it becomes problematic when applied to an urban population that includes people from very different cultural heritages. This application of culture to health-related programs at reservation settings also fails to incorporate the mechanism of informal social control which historically is one of the prime functions of culture.

One result of colonization has been the weakening of traditional methods of social control by Native American communities over their members. May (1982) has asserted that the susceptibility of various Native American groups to alcohol-related problems is correlated with the amount of social disintegration of culture. Tribes with high traditional integration and low acculturation stress experience much lower levels of alcohol- and drug-related problems than tribes with high acculturation stress and low traditional integrations. While acculturation stress and the destruction of traditional tribal economies contribute to alcohol-related problems, the weakening of informal control mechanism by loss of culture has not been adequately investigated. One uninvestigated use of culture, then, would be to strengthen those mechanisms within the culture which work to sanction or control what is consensually considered acceptable or deviant behavior. This implies increased autonomy and authority for tribal leaders and a systematic intentional revitalization of traditional culture.

This approach has had tremendous success with one tribe in British Columbia (Guillory, Willie, and Duran 1988). The Alkali Lake band of the Shuswap Native Americans was able to decrease its alcoholism rate from 95 percent to 5 percent in ten years by "creating a community culture which no longer tolerated alcoholism as individual behavior, while concurrently revitalizing traditional culture" (1988, p. 30). The Tribal leaders assumed their legitimate authority to govern by formal and informal mechanism that proved to be one link in the solution to the alcohol problem. This approach necessitates redefinition of current notions of the participation of Native Americans in health care programs into the need for self-determination and control.

The preceding critique of the literature sets the stage for a discussion of the relevance of previous research as that research activity structures most intervention and prevention programs. It is well known that most of those programs have ended in failure, and recidivism rates in treatment programs are as high as they have always been. Most prevention projects are suspect in that prevention cannot be a rational process when the community is already inundated by alcoholism and substance abuse. Yet there are those institutions and funding agencies that continue to follow the avant garde mentality in funding programs that supposedly are preventing something that has already happened. The absurdity of this reasoning defies all sensibilities and is testimony to the degree to which most institutions are out of touch with the real problems facing the Native American community. The above discussion is given in orthodox academic format is so that the reader can contrast existing academic rhetoric with a postcolonial discussion of the same problem.

Postcolonial Discussion

Alcoholism and alcohol-related problems are seen by many health care providers, tribal leaders, and IHS officials as among the leading public health problems of contemporary Native American life. The psychological, physiological, and spiritual toll alcoholism takes on various tribes in terms of direct alcohol mortality cannot be disputed. In addition to deaths from alcoholism, alcohol psychoses, and cirrhosis of the liver, alcohol is thought to be a contributing factor in other high rates of death from causes such as suicide, homicide, and accidents. However, a review of the existing literature on the subject of Native Americans and alcohol contains gross inconsistencies between what is considered by many to be the genesis of the problem and suggestions for its amelioration. In addition, all but a few authors maintain a definition of the problem that masks the issues of domination and subjugation, issues which must be considered given the historical context of this problem.

We believe that the answers to the problem of alcohol existed and continues to exist within the Native American community, and practitioners must search within the traditional teachings and processes in order to address the problem in a more relevant manner. By adhering to Native American thought as much as possible, we also want to make the point that Native American people have produced and continue to produce legitimate and valid knowledge, although at times Native American knowledge is considered invalid by those who only see it through the lens of Western logical positivism.

The Theme of Alcohol in Native Social Movements

We are what we imagine. Our very existence consists in our imagination of ourselves.

—N. Scott Momaday

The impetus behind every ontological theory of disease undoubtedly derives from therapeutic need.

—George Canguilhem

Since the inception of the United States, governmental agencies, voluntary organizations, and academic projects have focused on the "plight" of the "Indian" (Deloria 1969). To focus on "Indians" without qualifications is to reinscribe an arbitrary category and a European invention (Berkhoffer, 1978). In 1492, more cultural and linguistic diversity existed on this continent than in Europe. The difference between tribes still accounts for 50 percent of American cultural diversity (Hodgkenson 1990). Nonetheless, not the least of the aforementioned concern has been directed at the effects of what has been labeled the unique style of native drinking.

Alcoholism and alcohol-related morbidity and mortality have been identified as major problems among "Indians" of North

America. Everett Rhoades, outgoing director of the Indian Health Services, states that "Alcohol misuse underlies many major causes of Indian deaths in reservation states and contributes to an array of physical conditions treated by the IHS. Four of the top 10 causes of death among Indians are alcohol related; injuries (18 percent of all deaths), chronic liver disease (5 percent) suicide (3 percent) and homicide (3 percent)" (1987, p. 464).

The images and identities of tribal people and the meaning and significance of alcohol in those constructions is the site of half a millennium of struggle between natives and others. The focus of the struggle is not the undisputable fact of excess alcohol-related problems or the necessity of intervention, issues in which tribal people have more concern and interest than any others. Rather, the struggle is over the sign "Indian" as a signifier of ethnicity, cultural traditions, a similar historical experience, or certain aesthetic preferences versus a stage in a social evolutionary ladder, the embodiment of a genetic wholism or degeneracy, a psychological archetype, or a shadow projection of an entire continent. This overdetermined and overloaded sign was and is always more and less than real tribal people could ever hope or dread to be. Within American popular and expert culture, Indianness is more than an ethnic assignment (like Italian or Irish) and to be a real Indian one must fit one of the binary oppositions or cease to be. Within this field of meaning, the nineteenth- and twentieth-century white reformers—the friends of the indian—were correct to exhort their members to "kill the Indian and save the man" (sic) (Harmon 1989).

It is our contention that alcohol-related behavior for many Native Americans is determined, in part, by the need to ascribe to this overloaded sign in all of its negative and positive associations in order to be recognized as Indian.

Native identity in its negative invention was inscribed with alcohol through colonial discourse as a means to depict all the irrationality, instinct, and intuition that the imagined colonial America was not. This projection was a multipurpose political and cultural move toward the production of a national American culture (Fox 1990). Native social movements from the seventeenth century to the present have fought colonial invaders, intrusive governmental policies, hegemonic social science, and popular culture to erase that inscription and for control over the sign, sometimes to reinscribe the positive stereotype (auto-Indianist) but sometimes to break out of the antagonism of binary opposites. Tribal and pan-native alcohol treatment and prevention programs have implicitly acknowledged the alcohol/identity association by their focus on the transformation of identity as a key theme. Often these acknowledgments, however, do not go far enough beyond Eurocentric stereotypes.

The intent of this discussion is threefold. First, we uncover the construction of the "drunk Indian" by briefly reviewing and critiquing public health research and prevention studies that exemplify native alcohol-related topics. By construction of "Indian," we are referring to "a cultural and ideological composite *Other* constructed through diverse representational discourses (scientific, literary, juridical, linguistic, cinematic, etc.)" versus the real people of indigenous descent who are material subjects of their histories in all their glorious specificity. This section of this chapter draws upon new critical scholarship in cultural studies, anthropology, and feminist studies by postcolonial and postmodern theorists.

Second, we trace the history of the concept of the "drunk Indian" through an examination of colonial discourse. By "colonial discourse" we mean the scientific and specialist writing and their associated worldview that served an important part in the imperialist endeavor to colonize the Americas and, in the process, constructed the stereotype of the "drunk Indian."

We then attempt an "effective history" (albeit far from being the only possible history) of tribal peoples and alcohol. This history—admittedly slanted toward affirming native agency, subjectivity, and resistance—employs discourse of native social movements of the eighteenth and nineteenth centuries to uncover a subjugated perspective on alcohol. We focus on three movements; the Long House Religion of Handsome Lake; the pan-Indian spiritual component of Tecumseh's struggle organized by his brother Tenskwatawa; and the inception and spread of the Native American Church in the United States. This brief overview of historical events is itself an intervention, albeit a theoretical one, in that it "starts from an intolerable present situation and then invents a genealogy of that situation that serves as a means for transforming the present" (Bogue 1989, p. 161).

Skepticism concerning the applicability of a purely medical or behavioral model to represent alcohol-related problems for native peoples does not deny the need or contribution of medicine or public health in the prevention or treatment of alcohol-related problems. The purpose here is to look deeper into the multidimensional nature of this problem for fresh perspectives and empowering interventions and not privilege a universalistic scientific discourse over the voice of the subject.

Hegemonic Discourse: Social Scientific Approaches to Indian Alcohol-Related Problems

Recent philosophical and scientific advances counsel us that theories do not mirror or correspond to reality; at best they are tools. This realization opens up space for investigation into not what is but what works. Sociocultural, behavioral, and disease theories are the leading lenses that public and Indian health officials apply to interpret and assuage harmful patterns of alcohol-related behavior. These approaches, however useful, are not neutral insights and assessments of native drinking patterns but rather venture to explain and predict behavior based on a very historically and culturally specific mode of representation—realism—which erroneously assumes unity between the sensible and intelligible. Embedded within this Eurocentric mode of representation is a biased assessment of non-Western cultures. Behavioral theories decontextualize and individualize social problems and many sociocultural theories continue European representations of native peoples that have origins in the politics of the colonial and early American era. Insofar as these approaches are cultural products—a form of literature—we can say that they are hegemonic. By this we mean that they partake in ideological/cultural domination by the assertion of universality and neutrality and by the disavowal all other cultural forms or interpretations.

Alcohol-related behaviors are partially derived from these omissions and representations that construct a monolithic native subject and inscribe this subjectivity/identity with powerlessness and deviance. For these reasons, sociocultural and behavioral theories of alcohol use are not sufficient to inform a strategy with the potential to overcome alcohol-specific and other damaging health behaviors. Most standard theories of alcohol problems assume an evolutionary anthropology, a sociology of underdevelopment, or a pathologized psychology and target lifeworlds (culture) for behavioral change toward "normal" (read: western European). Programmatic failures in either participation or behavioral change should include an interpretation of target population resistance to cultural and/or social manipulation.

A Double Deconstruction: Indian Alcoholics

In her much-cited work *Firewater Myths* (1976), J. Leland undertakes a literature review to determine the extent of alcohol addiction among Indians. She endeavors to discern the presence of the forty-three categories of E. M. Jellinek's symptoms of alcohol addiction in 241 published reports of research investigating native people of numerous tribal and community affiliations. The commonality of the articles, Leland reports, are that in some way they discuss the use of alcohol among the populations under investigation. Within thirty-six of the forty-three categories, insufficient evidence existed to determine the presence or absence of a particular symptom of alcohol addiction. By Leland's assessment, however, there was enough evidence to determine the presence of (a) an "avid" drinking style, (b) alcoholic cirrhosis, and (c) prolonged intoxification; the absence of (d) guilt feelings about drinking behavior and (e) social pressure not to drink; and conflicting evidence about (f) aggressive behavior, (g) solitary drinking, and (h) reinterpretation of interpersonal relations. Leland's conclusions question the reified concept of alcoholism more than they provide any definitive knowledge about alcohol and native peoples. Her critique asserts a territorial and methodological imperative: Native drinking patterns and the presence or absence of related problems must be considered within emic categories and anthropologists are best suited for that work.

Leland pinpoints an important problem in applying the label "disease" to alcohol-related behavior within an Indian population. The disease theory presents alcohol-related problems ahistorically and within the paradigm of the medicalization of a social problem (Room 1984). This conceptual medicalization, which emerged in the postprohibition era, asserts that alcoholism is a disease to which only certain people are vulnerable (Fingarette 1988). In this disease framework, the contexualization of the problem is unnecessary and irrelevant. "Background, environment, race, sex, social status—these make no appreciable difference when once the disease takes hold of the individual. For all intents and purposes he might as well then be labelled with a number: he has become just another victim of the disease of alcoholism" (Mann, in Fingarette 1988, p. 2).

The array of concepts and categories delineated in Jellinek's theory (albeit the first generation of its construction) are presented, from a medical perspective, as a true and neutral picture of Indian alcohol problems. A close reading, however, uncovers the assumptions and language of a functionalist and binary view of social problems: lack of socialization into the correct meaning and use of alcohol as measured against the standard of the dominant culture. The seemingly objective methodological tools in this genre of behavioral investigation simultaneously construct the pathological subject as well as its inverse. The categories of analysis reflect an opposition between an idealized subject, well integrated and normalized into correct alcohol use, and those who for a variety of reasons, including some individual genetic factor X, incomplete modernization, psychological pathology, or resistance, fail or refuse to strive for inclusion into this idealized, neutral society. If *alcoholic* as a term means the inability to live up to an idealized Madison Avenue construct of success or beauty; if it signifies periodic psychological pathology, family dsyfunction, or general feeling of anomie, then alcoholism is actually the more frequent condition in our world and should therefore be considered the norm.

This approach to alcohol-related problems, both the crystallization of the disease entity and the assumption of the neutral subject, carry implicit suppositions about the self and scientific methodology which are presently contested. It operates within an a priori, essentialist Cartesian model of a unified, rational, autonomous subject, the construction of which is philosophically dead (Lash and Freidman 1992). "In short, the epistemological and moral subject has been definitively decentered, the conception of reason linked to it irrevocably desublimated. Subjectivity and intentionality are not prior to but a function of forms of life and systems of language; they not only 'constitute' the world but are themselves elements of a linguistically disclosed world" (Baynes, Bowman, and McCarthy 1987). Postcolonial scholars posit a decentered self: "that which operates as a subject may be part of an immense discontinuous network ('text' in the general sense) of strands that may be termed politics, ideology, economics, history, sexuality, language and so on" (Guha and Spivak 1988, p. 13).

The medical model of alcoholism deproblematizes the material history of science as well. Foucault, in *The Birth of the Clinic* (1973), brilliantly dissected what he called "technologies of power" authorized by the sciences of medicine. He illustrates that, far from objective statements of truth, the science of medicine emerged fully implicated in practices of domination.

J. Trimble, A. Padilla, and R. Bell (1987), leading minority researchers, maintain that "there is no universal and all encompassing explanation for drug and alcohol abuse among American Indians" (p. 5). Factors that have been identified in health research as accounting for the high prevalence of substance abuse within this population include (a) cultural dislocation and lack of integration either into traditional Indian or western culture, (b) lack of clear-cut sanctions of use in the population, and (c) strong peer group pressure and support for inappropriate use (Bell 1988; Edwards and Edwards 1984; May 1982). In addition to these determinants, many researchers agree that substance-related problems can be attributed partly to poverty, poor school adjustment and failure, unemployment, antisocial behavior, criminal arrest, increased morbidity and mortality, lack of opportunity, feelings of uncertainty, hopelessness and despair, and the family breakdown (Edwards and Edwards 1984; Schinke, Bebel, et al. 1988; Schinke, Orlandi, et al. 1988; Trimble 1984).

By positing a lack of socialization into either Indian or Western culture, Trimble, Padilla, and Bell assume a pan-Indian culture or a tribal culture as immediately transparent, the positive stereotype. They fall prey to a static view of culture and disavow the changing contingent nature of postmodern society. Williams offers a concept of culture that includes a critique of their lack of socialization argument:

> Among human beings new cultural forms are continually created out of anything available and suitable to the material and intellectual problems confronted by members of the population. All members of a population take part, albeit not the same part, in ordering, reordering, and supplementing the elements (for example, materials, actions, ideas, and interpretations) necessary to create new cultural forms or to maintain old ones. Some of these creations are categorized as mere adaptive strategies, everyday practices, superstitions, and deviant behavior, or otherwise labeled to indicate that they are not "real culture." (Williams 1990, p. 115)

In addition to alcohol-related problems, many of the well-intentioned researchers find deviance and powerlessness in their investigations of Indian life-styles and subjectivity. In addition, these findings, as in the case of the Indian alcoholic, conversely construct an objective norm—the approximation of which measures health. The problem for native peoples is that this norm looks surprisingly like an idealized European American cultural life-style and worldview.

Evidence against a purely medical model of alcoholism is also found in sociocultural scholarship on drinking. Inconsistent and incompatible definitions of alcoholism, as well as a large degree of cultural variation regarding what constitutes an alcohol problem indicate that the constellation of outcomes associated with alcohol consumption are not fully explored within a medical framework.

Indisputable (albeit differing) associations of alcohol with Indian identity have been found and noted by numerous anthropologists. Nancy Lurie (1979), a well-published academic authority on certain aspects of Indian culture including the use of alcohol, cites her own and colleague's ethnographic research to assert that native drinking is (a) not necessarily dysfunctional from a native viewpoint, (b) a way for the individual and community to identity as Indian, particularly for mixed breeds, and (c) a form of protest against white Americans and middle-class norms. Lurie feels native people know "the value of negative stereotype as a form of communication and protest demonstration to register opposition and hold the line against what they do not want until they can get what they do want." In her opinion, drinking is used consciously or unconsciously by native people to resist efforts at integration or acculturation and may serve a broad collective purpose as well as an individual one.

Good intentions and ethnographic expertise aside, Lurie reinscribes a monolithic Indian identity and reaffirms the image of the noble savage rather than recognizing tribal status as an ethnic origin. She asserts that "recorded in earliest documents . . . [and] still noted in contemporary field notes" are the Indian values. These include "beliefs that one should take full responsibility for his own actions, to exhibit concern for personnel dignity, to take pride in resourcefulness and to adopt what is at hand in order to survive"(1979, p. 144).

Vine Deloria, scholar and political activist, uses a syllogism to explain the identity/alcohol association. He states, "young Indians were sold the notion by anthropologists that Indians live in two worlds; people who live in two worlds drink; therefore, to be real Indians they must drink" (Lurie 1979, p. 144).

In another study, Richard Robbins (1992) investigates the use of alcohol in "identity resolving forums" among the Naskapi located on the Quebec-Labrador border. Robbins finds that people who have jobs are happy drunks and brag around, whereas people who do not have jobs exhibit more aggressive behavior and try to get the people with jobs to acknowledge that they're still their friends and still part of the group. Furthermore, Robbins found that the more there are identity struggles, the more that identity resolving forums involving alcohol will be held for resolution. Robbins inadvertently demonstrates, through its necessary use in identity resolving forums that alcohol use affirms Indian identity for the Naskapi.

A question arises as to the use of cultural information in alleviating alcohol-related problems in Indian country. The national Office (Center) for Substance Abuse Prevention exhorts alcohol and drug program evaluators to become culturally competent, in part, to "increase an evaluator's ability to collect, analyze and disseminate accurate and useful information" (1992, p. 59). Taussig, a prominent critical anthropologist specialist in the forms of native peoples oppression, asserts that rather than efforts to make the field more relevant to its multicultural audience, "experts will avail themselves of that [cultural] knowledge only to make the science of human management all the more powerful and coercive" (1992, p. 106).

Recent critical movements within the human sciences have made efforts to transcend the ideological baggage of scholarship in the service of empire. Postmodern critics of colonial discourse have moved from studying colonial history to studying the history of colonial knowledges.

Colonial Discourse: Indians and Alcohol

The last twenty years have seen some very significant advances in theoretical and empirical investigations of oppression and domination, specifically by postcolonial and cultural studies scholars, French poststructuralists and the German critical theorists (Derrida 1980; Habermas 1987). The terms *colonialism, colonize,* and *colonial discourse* have been used by these scholars to signify similar processes and effects occurring in different historical times and at different analytical levels. Most Native American populations in the United States have been subjected to all or a combination of these processes.

Edward Said, a leading postcolonial scholar, defines colonialism as an effect of imperialism that results in settlements on distant territories. Imperialism means the "practice, the theory, and the attitudes of a dominating metropolitan center" (Said 1993, p. 9). The association of native peoples with alcohol occurred within the context of colonial discourse. Homi Bhabha (1983) defines colonial discourse as an apparatus of power that strategically creates a space for a subject people through the production of knowledges by colonizer and colonized which are stereotypical but antithetically evaluated. Its mechanism is the scientific, moral, or aesthetic writing and other representation which create the foundation and rationale for the colonial political and economic agenda.

JanMohamed characterizes colonialist writing as representation of a "world at the boundaries of 'civilization', a world that has not (yet) been domesticated by European signification or codified in detail by its ideology" (1985, p. 83). In our analysis, colonial discourse is identified by the institutions to which it relates and by the position from which it comes and which it marks out for the speaker. That position does not exist by itself, however, but is best understood as a standpoint taken up by the discourse through its relation to another, ultimately opposing, discourse (Macdonell 1986).

The Wild Man

The image of the native as the exotic other already existed in European culture before Columbus's initial journey (analogous to our current imaginings and obsessions with extraterrestrials). Within the numerous mythical characters in European stories and drawings in the Middle Ages, a certain genre appeared whose figures had in common their role as the negative self-definition of European nonpopular culture. The roots of the projected image of the American Indian are found in one of these symbols, the wild man (Berkhoffer 1978; Mason 1990).

The significance of the wild man was profound in the Middle Ages. It symbolized pure European alterity and everything which eluded the normalizing gaze of the church. The image of the wild man referred to what was "uncanny, unruly, raw, unpredictable, foreign, uncultured, and uncultivated. . . . Man in his unreconstructed state, faraway nations, and savage creatures at home thus came to share the same essential quality" (Berkhoffer 1978, p. 3). Colins (1987) contends that at least the first twenty pictorial images seeking to present Native Americans are of this image. Most were created in the fifty years after Colomubus's initial journey, and all are ethnographically incorrect depicting native men with long flowing beards accompanied by various monstrous forms of life.

The earliest images of native peoples in the European imagination reveal the projection of European binary alterity and ambivalence. The images that any one individual or group chose to represent native peoples told more about their own ideology vis-à-vis modernity than it did about their knowledge or attitude toward real native people (Hulme 1990). Representations of indigenous peoples were social commentary. The savage wild man provided the comparison necessary for a celebration of an illustrious European civilization as the pinnacle of social evolution and provided the ideological foundation for the Christian civilizing mission of imperialist culture. Contrarily, the positive noble savage stereotype, who was at one with nature and in touch with his instinctual self, negatively assessed Europe's burgeoning capitalist discipline and reason's iron cage envelopment of more traditional forms of life.

The imagery of the drunken native—violent, lawless, impetuous—emerges clearly in this analysis as one of the instruments which attuned Western collective consciousness to the notion of a North America awaiting the civilizing and rationalizing mission of European settlement. The most striking thing about the wild man archetype in Western art and literature is that after having been one of the most frequently depicted themes in the fourteenth and fifteenth centuries, it "disappeared from the visual arts and literature by the end of the [16th] century" (Colins 1987, p. 29). The image left European art and literature and came to rest squarely on the shoulders of America's tribal peoples.

An Oppositional Identity

The association of certain Native American groups with a destructive use of alcohol, the drunk Indian stereotype, dates to the late seventeenth and eighteenth centuries, when European settlements were established in North America. The development and spread of this image paralleled the development and spread of the concept of reason as it came to be embodied in the state replacing church and monarchical dictates as the guiding principle in European social organization (in the Enlightenment) (MacAndrew and Edgerton 1969).

One of the many possible historical stories to tell about Native American communities and alcohol is, in part, a story about the power to define, produce, and disseminate meaning. It is about the nature of alterity and a culturally and historically specific form of (European) reason that constructs identity on the boundaries of what it is not, therefore constructing what it is. It is about marginalized groups of people who are objects of an attribution of identity and history and about the agency of those groups in resisting and generating counterhegemonic meaning. It is about a struggle to be subjects rather than objects of history and science. It is about the location, mode, and idiom of cultural articulation.

The definition and significance of alcohol is centered around the struggle of related terms and their binary opposites: tradition/assimilation and savagery/civilization. Alcohol was used as a metonomy by both sides of a power struggle to define both the meaning and value of Indian versus white identity and the moral grounding and guiding principles of the colonization.

> First, those of the *English* giving: as *Natives, Savages, Indians, Wild-Men*, (so the Dutch call them *Wilden*) *Abergeny men, Pagans, Barbarians, Heathen*.
>
> Secondly, their *Names*, which they give themselves.
>
> I cannot observe that they ever had (before the coming of the *English, French* or *Dutch* amongst them) any Names to difference themselves from strangers, for they knew none. . . .
>
> They have often asked mee (*sic*), why we call them *Indians*, Natives, &c. And understanding the reason, **they will call themselves *Indians*, in opposition to *English***, &c. (Roger Williams, 1643, as quoted in Berkhoffer 1978, p. 15)

Colonial Ideology: Benjamin Rush and Indian Tom

European colonial logic universalizes the Western liberal discourse of civility to justify its authority while simultaneously denying the applicability of civility to native people. This subterfuge of logic is overtly and un-selfconsciously used by Benjamin Rush, one of the primary thinkers of the American Enlightenment, a member of the Continental Congress, a signer of the Declaration of Independence, a powerful educator, a philosopher of republican ideology, one of the major architects of American nationalist ideology, and a voluminous writer.

In his biography written in 1793 (1948 edition cited herein), Rush shares the insights on civility he acquired while on extended medical apprenticeship in Europe between 1761 and 1766. During his time in Paris, he observed many similarities between French culture, "the most civilized of any nation in the world," and the "savages" of North America. The French and Indian cultures, he notes, share a lack of "delicacy in the intercourse of the sexes with each other" in that both French and Indian women do not conceal their sexual desires or needs from their men. The French are fond of "ornamenting their faces with paint, so are the Indians." Natives and French both eat their primary meal in the evening; in both races the people of means are fond of fishing and hunting; and the Indian and French seldom address each other by proper names. In addition, both cultures hold laborious occupations in contempt and highly regard the military arts. From these observations Rush deduces that there is a circular course in the progression from savagery to civility and notes that "the highest degrees of civilization border upon the savage life" (1948, p. 71). For Rush, the similarities in culture between the French and native could no sooner attribute civility to tribal peoples than could his culture admit thievery and genocide.

Rush, in his role as medical educator that would subsequently earn him the title of father of American psychiatry, had occasion to deliver a paper in 1774 to colleagues in Philadelphia entitled *An Enquiry into the Natural History of Medicine among the Indians of North America and a Comparative View of Their Dis-*

eases and Remedies, with those of Civilized Nations (1948). During the course of this talk, he expounded on the vices common to the Indians of North America. In addition to uncleanness and idleness, the third most common vice Rush sites is drunkenness. Rush told his colleagues that drunkenness was part of the Indian character and that the savages glory in their fondness for strong liquor. He told the following tale:

> A country man who had dropt from his cart a keg of rum, rode back a few miles in hopes of finding it. On his way he met an Indian who lived in the neighborhood, whom he asked if he had seen his keg of rum on the road? The Indian laughed in his face and addressed him in the following words "What a fool you are to ask an Indian such a questions. Don't you see I am sober? Had I met with your keg, you would have found it empty on one side of the road and Indian Tom drunk and asleep on the other." (1948, p. 188)

Within this small description, we see the logic of colonial discourse at work. Indians, whose life-styles and cultures are incommensurable with colonial America's, are somehow transparent to Rush's medical gaze. In one short story and the construction of the composite Indian Tom, he ascribes cultural attributes, emotions, and feeling that typify his image of natives as thieves, drunks, and totally outside the boundaries of civilized relations. In his position as physician and republican philosopher, he speaks with the double authority of clinician and colonial administrator. Alcohol as a polysemic cultural artifact has played a profound role in the production, colonization, and subjection of native people both materially and symbolically.

The Political Economy of Alcohol and Legislative Discourse in Colonial America

Very few North American native cultures had experience with alcohol before the first wave of European colonization. The Papago and Zuni used alcohol sparingly for either informal secular gatherings or in religious ceremonies. Within these circumstances, its use and effects were rigidly socially controlled and alcohol did not create social problems. The same is true for Natives of Central and South America, where the pre-Columbian use of alcohol was more widespread. Intoxication by alcohol was subject to strict prescriptive cultural traditions and did not interfere with tribal life.

Alcohol was introduced to North American Indian tribal communities by white explorers and traders. Jacques Cartier and Henry Hudson documented the first instances of alcohol used as a trading commodity in the late 1500s. Both men wrote that initially Indians were distrustful of the effects of alcohol but soon learned to enjoy the experience (MacAndrew and Edgerton 1969). Although alcohol was commonly used by explorers and traders as a means to establish friendship with native peoples, no early account indicates that Indians didn't become rowdy or in anyway suffered as a result.

Similar experiences were recorded for the initial contacts on the West Coast. In 1778, for example, Captain Cook reported that "when offered spirituous liquors, they rejected them as something unnatural and disgusting to the palate" (MacAndrew and Edgerton 1969). However, as Indians learned to enjoy the feeling of intoxification, liquor became a useful item for the explorers. As on the East Coast, no adverse effects of liquor were recorded during the earliest encounters.

This image changed, however, as white encroachment expanded. The explorers soon had to justify their travels by returning with valuable trading goods, particularly furs. The Indians were satisfied with trinkets and basic household goods initially; however, the tribes had only a limited demand for such items, and their curiosity and demand for them was soon fulfilled. Liquor then became one of the few trade items for which there was an increasing demand.

Alcoholic beverages became the ideal commodity for the conspicuous consumption that the traders needed to increase their business and profits. By the 1800s, liquor was the basic bartering item on the frontier, as the whites used deceitful tactics to make large profits. There are numerous reports of plying Indians with rum or whiskey as a show of friendship, then trading watered liquor of the most vile nature (often poisonous) for the valuable furs which Indians gave away while intoxicated.

As the liquor trade expanded, the "drunken Indian" stereotype was established. The Jesuits began to see brandy as their primary obstacle to converting Indians. They reported that natives turned into beasts when they drank and that debauchery, murder, and interfamily and intertribal feuds resulted. The traders themselves also documented the adverse effects of alcohol on their trading partners. John Long, a trader with the Chippewa between 1768 and 1782, reported that within ten days three men were killed and two wounded after a dreadful scene of riot and confusion occasioned by the effects of rum. Other trader accounts substantiate such observations; Indians were heavy drinkers, consumed large quantities in short periods of time, and often combined their drinking with bouts of violence and promiscuity (Winkler 1968).

This notorious behavior soon led to demands that the liquor trade end, first voiced by the Jesuits and later by the eastern colonialists who lived in well-established communities and towns. The popular image was that alcoholic beverages unleashed the basic savage nature of the otherwise noble natives; therefore, all Indians were totally incapable of holding their liquor and should not be allowed to drink.

Early colonial legislation, however, illustrates the contradiction between moralistic attitudes and economic benefit. Between 1643 and 1715, Pennsylvania, New York, New Hampshire, Maryland, Virginia, and Massachusetts all enacted statutes prohibiting the trade or sale of alcohol to Indians. Although early white settlements took measures to limit Indians' access to alcohol, legislative measures were continuously passed and repealed depending on the necessities of economic interests of the traders. These colonies as well as Ohio, Louisiana, Florida, and Maine all eventually outlawed the liquor trade targeted toward Indians, but all waited until after the most lucrative benefits had been attained.

Jacobs, in *Dispossessing the American Indian* (1972), reports an incident that illustrates frontier ambivalence. In 1756 Edmond Atkins, the English superintendent for the southern region of the frontier, recommended that heavy penalties be levied if a trader allowed an Indian to become drunk and that all liquor be watered. The commander-in-chief of the British force agreed and did "everything he could" to suppress the rum trade. However, as William Johnson, the northern superintendent, noted, these efforts were ill fated since the rum trade was an "absolute necessity" for the economy of the area (1954, p. 305).

The first federal legislation concerning Indian drinking was passed in 1802 as part of an act that established control of trade and intercourse with the Indian tribes. It read: "The President of the United States [is] authorized to take such measures, from time to time, as to him may appear expedient to prevent or restrain the vending or distributing of spirituous liquors among the all or any of the . . . Indian tribes" (Mosher 1975, p. 8). This prohibition, however, proved fruitless in the western frontier. Lemert reports that on the West Coast no attempt to control the liquor trade was made until the 1850s. The Supreme Court itself acknowledged the failure in an 1876 decision:

> It may be that the policy of the government on the subject of Indian affairs has, in some particulars, justly provoked criticism; but it cannot be said, that there has not been proper effort, by legislation and treaty, to secure Indian communities against the debasing influence of spirituous liquors. The evils from this source were felt at an early day, and in order to promote welfare of the Indians, as well as our political interests, laws were passed and treaties framed, restricting the introduction of liquors among them. That these laws and treaties have not always secured the desired result, is owing more to the force or circumstances which the government could not control, than to an unwillingness to execute them. Traffic with Indians is so profitable, that white men are constantly encroaching on Indian Territory to engage in it. (Mosher 1975, p. 9)

While there was considerable legislative activity concerning Indian drinking during the early years of white settlement, the liquor trade was not effected significantly; in fact, the legislatures were more concerned with protecting the trade as a valuable resource. The laws attempted to control practical concerns, such as prevention of war, colonial annoyances, or central control of a profitable trade, or reflected attempts to impose white religious and moral codes of behavior, but any legislation that interfered with the economic benefits of the liquor trade was not effectively enforced. Native drinking, despite all statement to the contrary, was encouraged to increase profit of the trade, to induce concessions, and to sap the strength of the tribes. Benjamin Franklin noted this final, most unspoken purpose: "And, indeed, if it be the design of Providence to extirpate these savages in order to make room for the cultivators of the earth, it seems not improbable that rum may be the appointed means. It has already annihilated all the tribes who formerly inhabited the seacoast" (Mosher 1975, p. 13).

While an overview of early American drinking legislation provides insight into the motivation behind the introduction of alcohol into Indian societies, alleged patterns of Indian drinking, and Indian/white relations, it does not provide a native interpretation of alcohol-related problems. One way to investigate the early function and meaning of alcohol for tribal societies is through an inquiry into its place as a theme in historical Indian social movements.

Indigenous Alcohol Discourse

Many alcohol prevention and treatment programs under native control have consciously or unconsciously overcome the inherent biases of standard human science approaches by employing indigenous theory (Weeks 1990). Indigenization refers to the replacement of Eurocentric models with local, native idioms (Atal 1981; Slagle and Weibel-Orlando 1986). Indigenous theory is an advance in treatment and prevention ideology for Native Americans in two ways. First, it utilizes knowledges and idioms produced by native people from within native culture, thus creating native subjects (those who know and act) rather than objects (those who are know and acted upon) of scientific and programmatic discourse. Second, this form of self-representation compels reflexivity, insight, and agency (*conscientização*).[1] This indigenization as it is applied to alcohol prevention and treatment can be interpreted as the legacy of social movement struggles of eighteenth-, nineteenth-, and twentieth-century native groups which produced alternative understandings of alcohol in Indian country. Indigenous approaches to prevention and treatment benefit by being accompanied by postcolonial histories of alcohol in Indian country. By postcolonial we mean the use of "a social criticism that bears witness to those unequal and uneven processes of representation by which the historical experience of the once-colonized comes to be framed in the West" (Bhabbha 1991, p. 63). A postcolonial history of alcohol situates the emergence of alcohol-related problems within the phenomena of colonial discourse (a primary strategy of colonialism) and the struggle over material and symbolic control of clashing economic and cultural traditions.

Counterhegemonic Discourse:
The Theme of Alcohol in Eighteenth- and Nineteenth-Century Native American Social Movements

Edward Said (1993) eloquently notes that the United States was forged out of numerous histories, often in conflict and contradiction of each other. Many of those histories are now asking to be acknowledged for their rightful contribution to *an* American society but most profoundly so that communities of color, the poor, and all other/marginalized groups may view themselves differently.

Temperance has either been the major focal point or a dominant theme in many native social movements over the last two hundred years. The Handsome Lake religion, the teachings of the Shawnee prophet Tenskwatawa, and the spread of the Native American Church all had temperance as a major subject. Regardless of whether the movement was an attempt at cultural

---

1. "Conscientização" refers to learning to perceive social, political, and economic contradictions and to take action against the oppressive elements of reality. For more, see Freire (1990).

"revitalization" or had a more political agenda, or whether it was tribally specific or pan-native, alcohol has been a predominant theme in most native collective action since its arrival among natives of North America. The meaning of alcohol to native people, therefore, appears highly symbolic.

The inscription of alcohol-related problems within the case studies outlined below can be conceptualized as a "displacement" of the colonial discourse on alcohol at the time. A religious or spiritual idiom gave the movement leaders and participants a alternative framework to codify their problems and propose solutions. This section of the book outlines the temperance aspects of the social movements mentioned above in search of a native voice in the construction of alcohol-related problems.

Handsome Lake

Handsome Lake, the Seneca prophet, preached abstinence from alcohol as early as 1800. The political climate present at the time of Handsome Lake's vision provides clues to the struggle for alcohol's function and meaning. The colonists contended that they had not only won the Revolutionary War against Britain, but also a de facto war against all of Britain's allies in the struggle which included large segments of the Iroquois Confederacy. In the Treaty of Paris of 1783 the United States claimed that it now owned all native territory south of the Great Lakes and the St. Lawrence River and east of the Mississippi River. Treaties were yet to be signed with the native tribes, but peace was to be given to the Iroquois by the victor of war. The only matter for negotiation was what lands the tribes were allowed to keep. The newly formed government badly needed Iroquois land both to pay off the enormous debt incurred to soldiers fighting the war and to sell in order to pay off other debts incurred from the conflict. In addition to the motives of the state, private speculators saw the potential for great profit in selling native land to settlers. Frontiersmen, with long standing hate for victorious native fighters, also tried to procure as much native land as possible.

The resulting Treaty of Fort Stanwix of 1784 was a fraud. Native leaders were coerced at gunpoint into signing a document conceding large tracts of land. Many of the native delegates left before the treaty was signed. The inability of the delegates to adequately represent the interest of their tribes led to the disintegration of the original Iroquois Confederacy. Another association of western tribes was coalesced with continued loyalties to the British. Although the War of the Northwest Territory waged by this group of the Western Iroquois Confederacy put the tribes in a much better negotiating position with the government, many of the Mohawk members of the confederacy had already fled to Canada during the negotiations for the treaty of 1784, and other members of the traditional confederacy did not support the efforts of the Western Confederacy because of its British alliances.

It was within these events that the original confederacy lost considerable power as a representative of tribes and as a negotiator, and its members were assigned to reservations. The reservation confinement made it easier for religious organizations, especially the Quakers, to begin their project of native assimilation. With the support of tribal leadership, the Quakers proceeded to teach Western agriculture, carpentry, and Christianity to the bands of the confederacy confined to reservations. In response to these attempts to promote assimilation, the bands were split on generational lines. Older Seneca tired of fighting attempted to see the value of the new agricultural life-style. The younger men, angry at the older generation for conceding land, saw little merit in the white people's ways. It was within this conflicting tribal will that the Seneca prophet emerged.

Handsome Lake's visions, the ensuing religion, and the effects these had on the political and social life of the Iroquois Confederacy are considered a form of cultural revitalization. The precepts he taught can be divided into two chronological categories: the apocalyptic and social gospels. His first visions contained three interrelated themes: the imminence of world destruction; the definition of sin; and the prescription for salvation. Cosmic catastrophe was immanent unless tribal members took steps to forestall its occurrence. The overriding sin according to his prophecy was failure to believe in his vision which would remedy the other basic sins including drinking alcohol, witchcraft, love magic, abortion, and various other evil practices. The third principle of his vision, salvation, was accomplished by refraining from sin and by reinstating certain traditional social organizational and ceremonial practices.

There were three main themes to Handsome Lake's social gospel, which he preached from 1801 till his death in 1815. The first related to the use of alcohol.

> Good food is turned into evil drink. Now some have said that there is no harm in partaking of fermented liquids. Then let this plan be followed; let men gather in two parties, one having a feast of food, apples and corn, and the other have cider and whiskey. Let the parties be equally divided and matched and let them commence their feasting at the same time. When the feast is finished you will see those who drank the fermented juices murder one of their own party but not so with those who ate food only. (Wallace 1969, p. 278)

Temperance remained a prime concern throughout Handsome Lake's mission. As did other tribal leaders, he saw alcohol as the leading cause of social instability and therefore a leading cause of the inability of the Seneca to regroup after the reservation confinement. The enactment of temperance was not left to individual conscience but was instituted in the political structure of several communities of the Great League itself. The liquor trade was outlawed by Corn Planter and other village chiefs of the Seneca. Handsome Lake was praised as being principally responsible for curing the Seneca of "the misuse of that dreadful manbane, distilled spirits" (Wallace 1969, p. 00)

The second social principle was peace and social unity. This principle was institutionalized in 1801 when Handsome Lake became the moral censor and principal leader of the Six Nations. His position toward whites was a cautious nationalism: peace toward the whites, in a separate but equal framework, and unity among the tribe and confederacy (Pan-nativism).

The third principle was the preservation of the tribe's land base. He was adamantly opposed to any further land concessions but promoted profitable exchanges of land that would geographically consolidate the confederacy's lands contributing to community control of disparate clans of the tribes.

The claim that Handsome Lake expanded the social gospel into a fourth principle, acculturation, is a misunderstanding of his intentions for white education. "Now let the Council appoint twelve people to study, two from each nation of the six. So many white people are about you that you must study to know their ways" (Wallace 1969, p. 278). Handsome Lake saw the value of obtaining a white education not in the socialization process that advanced assimilation to white values and culture, but in its promise of an equal negotiating position that would enable the members of the confederacy to retain their unique cultural lifestyle and economic land base. His mission, understood within the milieu of colonial oppression, was more nationalist than assimilationist.

The symbolic meaning of alcohol to Handsome Lake and other Confederacy leaders who were trying to maintain their culture amidst white economic, religious, and cultural intrusion can be gleaned from temperance's prominent place among other prescriptions for tribal revitalization. Handsome Lake taught that temperance from alcohol was as important as traditional ceremony, social organization, and maintenance of a land base to the continuity of tribal life for the Seneca and the Iroquois Confederacy.

Tenskwatawa, the Shawnee Prophet

Tenskwatawa emerged as a leading visionary of the Shawnee and neighboring tribes during a time of intense cultural change and from a personal life of great hardship. Originally named Lalawethika, the prophet was born fatherless in 1775. His mother, a despondent widow with eight children, abandoned her Shawnee offspring and returned to her Cree relatives in 1779. Tenskwatawa was raised by his older sister and other Shawnee but is generally thought to have been ignored by any real parental figures.

Influenced by this early life of physical and emotional abandonment, Tenskwatawa grew into an alcoholic degenerate. After sporadic involvement with the tribe's warfare against the invading colonists, lead by his brother Tecumseh, Tenskwatawa finally found his calling while undergoing a type of apprenticeship with the clan's medicine man. After the death of his mentor and his failure to be recognized by the clan as the man's rightful successor, Tenskwatawa experienced a series of visions and a near-death experience initially thought to be brought about by an alcoholic stupor.

During his near-death experience, the Master of Life did not allow Tenskwatawa to enter heaven, but he was permitted to gaze on a paradise, which he described as follows: "a rich fertile country, abounding in game, fish, pleasant hunting grounds and fine corn fields, ... they could plant, hunt, or play at their usual games, and in all things could remain unchanged" (Wallace 1969, p. 33). According to his vision, not all Shawnee were allowed to enter this heaven. Unvirtuous men, allowed only a glimpse of this paradise, where confined to a lodge within which a large fire burned. The most wicked were turned to ashes and others stayed in this place until their sins were atoned. Unrepentant drunkards were particularly mentioned by the prophet. They were "forced to swallow molten lead until flames shot from their mouths and nostrils"(Wallace 1969, p. 33). Although this type of purgatory had redemptive qualities for some sinners, less-virtuous tribesmen who eventually ascended to heaven never fully took part in the enjoyments of their more virtuous brothers. It was at this and another series of visions that Lalawethika was personally and socially transformed into the Shawnee prophet Tenskwatawa.

During the summer of 1805, the prophet and many Shawnee followers moved from their home at White River to establish a new settlement—Prophet's Town—in western Ohio. His teachings were similar to Handsome Lake's. First and foremost, Tenskwatawa denounced the drinking of alcohol as poison and accursed. In addition to denouncing the use of alcohol, he preached against the rising internal and external tribal violence, sexual promiscuity, and polygamous marriages.

The prophet, also like Handsome Lake, preached the return of certain traditional Shawnee ritual and ceremonial practices, although he also condemned certain practices and medicine men as corrupt and misguided. Tenskwatawa exhorted his fellow tribal members to give up their medicine bundles, which he claimed had lost their effectiveness. He substituted medicine sticks as a manifestation of personal power. Also similar to the Seneca prophet, Tenskwatawa urged tribal members to give up the notion of private property, to return to communal life, and to fight any white acquisition of native land. He instructed his followers to move away from using white people's food, technology, and manner of dress. While praising the traditional life of the Shawnee, Tenskwatawa warned against any close association with the colonial Americans. He went so far as to state that the Master of Life had informed him that the settlers were not made from him (the Master of Life) but were actually children of the evil spirit.

Tenskwatawa's teachings spread quickly among the tribes of Ohio. At the same time, federal attempts to gain native land through coerced and unfair treaty negotiations drove other tribal members, including some Chippewa, Mohican, Wyandot, Kickapoo, Potowatomi, Ottawas, Cree, and Assiniboin, into the prophet's camp. There is evidence that his doctrines had a large influence on native/white relations of the time. In 1807, for example, Captain Dunham, an American military commander on the Michigan frontier, heard complaints from traders that the Natives no longer accepted whiskey for trade and were refusing to discuss any further native land concessions (Edmunds 1983).

Eventually, Tenskwatawa's fate as a spiritual and cultural leader fell prey to the corrupt political manipulations of the encroaching white government and his own foray into the role of warrior. Unable to accommodate the hordes of followers flocking into Prophet's Town and unable to stop federally delegated "representative" tribal members from signing away native land, his mission, under his brother Tecumseh's guidance, turned more and more political. In November 1811 Tenskwatawa and his army of followers entered into and were defeated at the Battle of Tippecanoe. It was at this point that the prophet's influence reached its nadir.

The symbolic meaning of alcohol to Tenskwatawa and his followers can be concluded from the prominent place alcohol temperance was afforded in the prophet's doctrine. In this case, alcohol abstinence was the first precept taught. Alcohol was paramount among the evil white ways that natives would have to abandon in order to return to a state of equilibrium with the Master of Life and with fellow tribal members as well as with other tribes. Drinking alcohol, then, was associated with assimilation or the taking on of white culture. Drinking, like other white cultural artifacts, such as food and clothing, was condemned as a threat to native identity.

The Native American Church

Approximately seventy years after Handsome Lake and the Shawnee prophet provided the coalescence for pan-native collective action, another movement with strong temperance themes emerged. The peyote religion had its roots among the pre-Columbian natives of Mexico. Transported to natives north of the border by the Mescalero Apache in 1870, the religion quickly spread to the Kiowa and Comanche. Unlike the social movements of Handsome Lake and Tenskwatawa whose goal was revitalization, this movement is categorized as one of accommodation. It abandoned the messianic hopes of earlier movements and instead developed ideology and ceremonies more in line with the realities of native life in the early twentieth century. The Native American Church ceremony involves all-night meetings, usually held in a traditional native structure such as a tepee. In the ceremony participants sing and ingest peyote in order to cure themselves and to be closer to the Creator via the helper spirit, peyote. An early promoter of the religion stated, "The white man goes into his church house and talks about Jesus, but the Native goes into his tepee and talks to Jesus" (Hertzberg 1971).

Although the religion is not hostile toward Christianity, peyote groups differ in the amount of Christianity incorporated into the ceremony. Christian beliefs form the core rhetoric of some groups, whereas in others Christian references are absent.

One of the Native American Church's major canon is opposition to alcohol. Anthropologists studying native cultures have gone so far as to say that it began as a temperance movement with antialcohol activities not unlike the temperance movement in white society. Both movements originated at about the same time.

Two early missionaries of the Native American Church, Quanah Parker (Comanche) and John Wilson (Delaware/Caddo), both converted in the 1880s, typify the major strains of the religion that exist today. John Wilson attributed his cure from alcoholism to the assistance of the spirit of peyote. Wilson, while under the influence of peyote, had visions and received peyote songs, a body of moral and religious teaching, and details of ceremonial procedures. In these visions Wilson saw Christ and was told that at the time of his death he would be in the presence of both peyote and Christ. In contrast, Parkers' brand of peyotism had much less Christian influence. Both men, however, stressed right conduct, abstinence from alcohol, and peyote as a cure for disease.

Hertzberg (1971) has delineated twelve reasons why the Native American Church became the most successful pan-native movement, which today has members among almost all tribes. One important reason was the ability of the church to "cure" alcoholism, which contributed not only to individual stability and health but also to the stability and health of native communities.

Other Native Social Movements

The Ghost Dance religion, which started at approximately the same time as the peyote cult, had far fewer references to alcohol abstinence. Jack Wilson, the movement's prophet, however, is known to have specifically addressed the topic. In May 1917 an Inspector Dorrington from the Nevada Agency reported that Jack Wilson (Wovoka) was "advising the Natives to abstain from the use of all drugs and intoxicants" (Stewart 1977, p. 222).

The Native Shaker Church was founded during the second wave of native/white contact among the natives of the Northwest Coast and northern California regions in approximately 1889. The church is thought of as a response to acculturation pressure and the introduction of alcohol into the region. Native researchers contend that in addition to its function as a native religion, it functions as a "culture-based indigenous treatment response to alcohol misuse" (Slagle, Weibel-Orlando, p. 312) It is estimated that 76 percent of the religion's members are recovering alcoholics.

In all the social movements discussed above, alcohol carried a symbolic association as an artifact of assimilation. In both Handsome Lake's and Tenskwatawa's social reformation movements, formal and informal methods of social control sought to banish the use of alcohol from tribal life while simultaneously instituting "traditional" social interactions. For the Shawnee prophet, white people's food, clothing, and alcohol were to be abandoned for a return to more ancestral cultural artifacts. The cure of alcoholism and alcohol abstinence was for the most native of the social movements of its time, the peyote cult, one of its most important and prized features.

Social movements "work" insofar as they succeed in "strengthening tribal identity and distinctions between American Native and European populations" (Thornton 1986, p. 49). Native social movements as statements of identity and the prominence of alcohol within these movements clarifies a category of meaning for this substance. Alcohol historically is associated with Indian identity within native communities and among the broader dominant population. As either a hidden or conscious meaning, it is at the same time viewed by natives as destructive of native life and as a symbol of protest, as an affirmation of native identity.

Conclusion

Eurocentric conceptualizations of native alcohol-related problems may contribute to the ongoing reproduction of these same problems. Certainly, to the extent they have been evaluated, they have been found lacking as a form of prevention or treatment for people of indigenous descent who identify strongly as Indians.

Implicit in this critique is a call for indigenous models of etiology and intervention. Materials from colonial America trace an alternative, implicitly indigenous, etiology and intervention strategy of alcohol-related problems. We have used discourse from eighteenth- and nineteenth-century Indian social movements to begin formulating one (not the only) alternative strategy.

Standard social science research and practice toward this problem are hegemonic discourse and native etiologies and interventions are counterhegemonic. An investigation into indigenous approaches to treatment and prevention is needed to evaluate their effectiveness and to codify their belief system for a more comprehensive construction of alternative, workable Indian identities at this turn of the millinium.

"Indian," in its popular cultural meaning, is not an ethnicity but a stage in a social evolutionary ladder. This meaning precludes people of indigenous descent from ever living up to the image of Indianness and in the process inscribes a lost relations to nature or spiritual connectedness. People of indigenous descent must struggle to recapture our own mode of representation and go beyond Eurocentric stereotypes to invent a postcolonial identity imagining ourselves richly.

Clinical Issues from a Postcolonial Perspective

In this section we discuss the ancient thought presented earlier with contemporary traditional understanding of alcoholism. Through the integration of the old and new, along with modern clinical interventions based on this integration, we hope the reader can make the necessary leap from one century of Native American thinking to another without much dissonance.

Even though alcohol existed in Native American culture before the arrival of the Europeans, there were tribal controls and most alcohol consumption took place within a ceremonial context. This was also the case with other mind-altering substances, and continues to this day with the strict control of peyote for ceremonial purposes. The ritualistic control of the substance was and continues to be respected. To our knowledge there have been no cases of Native American people addicted to peyote. This illustrates that as long as the tribe and tradition delineate the appropriateness of a substance then the substance will not be abused.

Most reservations are dry, and yet alcoholism runs rampant in these communities. Alcohol was for the most part not used ceremoniously in most tribes that make up the United States today. The socialization process brought on by the frontier mentality and the systematic practice of making Native Americans drink until drunk has been well documented. The disruption of the family and other systemic and well-organized genocidal practices by the United States government are still reflected in the high death rates due to alcoholism in this country. What the soldiers did not destroy, the federal policy of termination is still destroying today through the massive death rate attributed to alcohol. Future generations are going to be affected regardless of what we do now because of the high incidence fetal alcohol syndrome.

The political authority of tribal chiefs was removed through the institution of the Indian Reorganization Act of 1932. The political and spiritual leadership of the tribe represented in the traditional structure became separated. Raymond reports:

> the power of the chiefs to maintain unwritten tribal law and tradition was removed. The people had spiritual leaders who had no power to control them. . . . The spiritual power and influence of the traditional community began to dissipate. It became subject to a type of tribal anarchy where families and individuals experienced the deterioration of traditional values and the disrespect of others became a matter of patience and tolerance for those affected. This had negative consequences for any transmission of a spiritual understanding of alcohol induced illness. (Raymond 1983, p. 30)

The systematic destruction of social control mechanisms within the tribal governing bodies is apparent in the high rates of health and social problems brought on by a continuance of the genocidal policy that the U.S. government continues to target toward Native American people.

Alcohol began by disrupting tribal life and traditional ways. In his research, Michael Raymond was able to acquire firsthand accounts of how Native American traditional leaders view the disruption of tradition:

> When alcohol came in it really started breaking up the old traditional ways of Canvas Dancing. The real old timers that reenacted this Canvas Dance in memory of their ancestors who went out to battle would continue to sing from tipi to tipi. A younger guy comes in and starts staggering around because he is drunk. He grabs hold of the buffalo robe and starts singing. Maybe the fellow standing next to him thinks the drunk is ruining it. So the next year he makes up his mind that he will not go and have to experience the same thing. This is what happened. Pretty soon it's all drunks that are around there. The old people who carry on the ceremony stay at home and stop participating. The drunks took the meaning out of what the people were doing. Today when the people go to the Canvas Dance they think they have to be drunk to do it. (Raymond 1983, p. 41)

The loss of the appropriate approach to tradition made explicit in the last sentence of the quote is saddening. Alcohol served to create a split within the community: traditional Native Americans use alcohol and traditional Native Americans do not sanction the use of alcohol. The above quote helps to illustrate this point in that some people have to be drunk in order to be involved in what they perceive as tradition, and there are those people who do not drink alcohol since they are part of traditional culture. According to Raymond:

> this means Traditional people who did not use alcohol must have maintained a sense of relation and community to sup-

port their values and beliefs. . . . It is a spiritual dilemma involving the struggle of tribal members to develop an identity congruent with a spiritual reality. It is a spiritual reality represented by the supernatural presence of ancestors and oral tribal teaching. It is a struggle of the individual to attain a spiritual role and strength that affirms himself as a positive representative of the warrior tradition. . . . it is a journey of the soul toward the sacred in the midst of the profane created by human beings. (1983, p. 50)

Traditional people also have a way to describe alcohol and the conceptualization of alcohol that differs from Westerners. Alcohol is perceived as a spiritual entity that has been very destructive of Native American ways of life. The alcohol "spirits" continually wage war within a spiritual arena and it is in the spiritual arena that the struggle continues. Raymond illustrates this point in a further talk with Arlee:

I have my beliefs about alcohol. It's an evil person that brought it in. The evil spirit. He is a being that is really out to get everybody. If he sees somebody doing good, he will try his best to break it up. He does not want anybody being good. He wants to break them down. I use myself as an example. I was trying to quit drinking and would be driving down the road. I had stopped drinking for three or four months. All of a sudden I will be tempted. It's like a little voice saying, "Why don't you stop off here and have a drink." Somebody may come to visit and ask you to go for a ride with them. They may stop at a bar and ask you to come in and have one. If you say no, then their reply is to ask you to have just one, because it won't hurt. You think to yourself that you can have one and you take it. That's all it needs. That's all the evil one has to do is get you to have on drink if you think it is wrong for you. He does not have to be with you all night and tempt you to have more drinks. He can go out and find somebody else. All he needs to do is drag you down once. (1983, p. 55)

In order to appreciate what is being said one must remember that this awareness is different than one coming from a Western cosmology. The Native American worldview does not have the compartmentalization that is found in Western ways of thinking. Instead, any dysfunction that occurs can be perceived as having an effect on the spiritual as well as psychological aspects of the totality. According to Raymond: "It is a perspective wherein alcohol use is interpreted as a spiritual illness, and illness whose contagion affects both spiritual communities existing on the reservation and determines the acts of its members" (1983, p. 60).

Alcohol also has had an effect on the way spiritual power and traditional medicine are used in a community. Traditionally, in order for the medicine to work there had to be an adherence to a traditional way of life on the part of the medicine person and the patient. Since alcohol is a violation of tradition, the use of traditional healing practices can place the medicine person, the client, and the community in jeopardy. Disrespect of tradition can be manifested in negative consequences, which are due to discord within the cosmology. No longer will the healing occur within the context of the seventh sacred direction. Instead, the whole community has shifted into an attitude that is out of balance, and in order to restore balance the community members must begin to live according to traditional rules.

Clinical Applications

When E.D. first started working with Native American people in a clinical setting, all he had as far as training was a Western master's degree in psychology and was in the process of obtaining a doctorate. He had no formal training in working with Native American people, although he had grown up hearing about traditional ways of living. At that time he was still heavily involved in explaining the world from a radical behavioral standpoint and was resistant to other psychological ways of seeing the world. The approach that he followed gave him a tidy package of the world and its phenomena—or at least so he thought.

During the last conversation E.D. had with his grandfather, his grandfather spent a lot of effort in telling him about processes of transformation. E.D. listened but did not know what his grandfather meant by all of his talk. E.D. actually wondered why his grandfather was taking this effort since talking was an effort to him at this time because he was on oxygen support. Shortly after that conversation, E.D. stumbled on *Symbols of Transformation* (1956), by Jung, which curiously had similarities to the last conversation with his grandfather.

During his second year of working on his Ph.D., E.D. was contacted by a Native American health agency and was asked to come in and talk about developing a mental health program. E.D. was interviewed and was offered a job in which he was to develop a mental health program. His first day of work told the story of how the process was to unfold. E.D. arrived at the office and asked where his office was, and the secretary replied "wherever you want it to be." He later asked the administrator what he was expected to do, and the administrator replied, "Whatever you want to do." There had never been a mental health program at the agency and E.D. was to develop one. Needless to say he was overwhelmed and the training that he had had up to that point soon proved to be useless. At that point E.D. started to search for meaningful material that would assist in the development of a meaningful and useful clinical approach.

To accomplish a relevant treatment process, the traditional way of healing encompasses symbol, myth, and ritual. E.D. realized that in order to find what the psyche needs emerging symbols and images had to be taken into account. It becomes necessary to find the meaning of ancient symbols to achieve relevance, and unconscious symbols need to be assimilated into consciousness. In order to understand the symbolic soul of Native Americans, it is necessary to look for soul in myths, symbols, and images. To facilitate the search for mythological material, we have used material from Mesoamerica which is abundant in catalogued relevant mythological material (Sejourne 1957).

From Mesoamerica the notion of the conjunction of fire and water existed as images projected by the psyche. One of the most archaic images is that of Tlaloc, who is related with water and at times also with fire. The deeper meaning that allowed for Tlaloc to emerge was that of the union of sun and rain producing life on the Earth. In a fresco at Teotihuacan we find Tlaloc as the god of rain with a solar flower emerging from his mouth, and in another image we find the god of fire known as Huehueteotl.

The union of opposites is apparent where the god of rain is seen with wings of a butterfly. According to Sejourne, fire is the symbol of both movement and well-being (swastika), which clearly indicates the union of opposites. The ancient mesoamerican psyche was preoccupied with the notion of uniting matter with spirit, or with the idea of being within the seventh sacred direction. The notion of union is once more seen when one considers the act of a major divinity, Quetzalcoatl. After becoming drunk and committing a violation of taboo, he threw himself into the fire and his heart emerged toward heaven (transformation through the destruction of matter or body).

Fire transforms matter in the ancient Native American psyche. The trophy that the warrior was after was the *atl-tlachinolli* (atl means water, tlachinolli means burnt), which is nothing else than his own soul. The union is such a basic notion that the Templo Mayor de Tenochitlan had the god of rain and the god of fire next to each other on the same pyramid.

It is apparent from these notions that the Native American psyche has derived meaning from the union of opposites and the undifferentiated search for conjunction. The lack of harmony may be one of the reasons why the a psyche is so fascinated by firewater (alcohol), instead of a balanced relationship with the center or the seventh sacred direction. The dual nature of the conjunction is close to one found in psychoanalytic thinking in the image of Mercurius, who personifies both the diabolical and the sacred simultaneously. The difficulty is in having the individual identify the positive or balanced aspect of the archetype. Once the positive aspect of the archetype has been identified, the task is to differentiate the positive aspect into the conscious awareness of life.

When the words "fire" and "water" are examined, it is obvious that they stand diametrically opposed to each other. Through the process of fermentation, the opposites are united to form a unity, as in the making of alcohol (the fire from the sun and the water used to grow the plant are united in the process of fermentation, thereby producing alcohol). Therefore, it is apparent that this union may serve as the object of projection for a psyche, particularly one which recently experienced a separation of opposites brought on by a psychic disaster or trauma (such as was experienced in the Spanish conquest).

The separation in the psyche happened when the colonizing people overwhelmed the psyche of the Native American through the forceful imposition of a mythology that was foreign and differentiated in a totally opposing cosmology. At the point of trauma the psyche may have attempted to regress in order to escape complete annihilation. Since total regression is impossible, the Native American psyche was left with some of the previous consciousness. If we were to look at the previous whole of the Native American psyche, we could see that it has become split. Part has regressed, but some of the psyche is still left with awareness. This small part of consciousness is totally impotent in the face of the overwhelming opposite mythological imposition, and therefore only serves as a place where the individual and collective Native American psyches can remain painfully aware of the overwhelming onslaught of the conquest, which literally rapes the psyche.

The Native American psyche then searches for an object onto which to project in order to restore harmony and relationship with the world. Not only will the psyche need a compensatory object, but the psyche will need an object which typifies the long-lost conjunction or relationship with the spiritual world. The firewater conjunction offers such an object, complete with the hermetic vessel in which the psyche can become contained as it anesthetizes itself into the illusion of being in harmony with the world once more. Unfortunately, the projection into the vessel is undifferentiated and unconscious, which immediately unleashes the shadow side of the compensatory object—the destructive power of alcohol. At this point the Native American psyche is contained in the bottle in what is literally a state of possession, which requires more alcohol to anesthetize the reality of the situation confronted. Thus the problem becomes a complete cycle in and of itself.

The firewater projection remains unconscious and therefore the small remaining consciousness becomes totally seduced and possessed by its own projection. This seduction and possession is made possible in part because while the unconscious is projected onto the object, the object is in turn introjected by the ego. This introjection, in turn, gives the object (alcohol) the quality of being a live part of the projected psyche. Therefore, the firewater becomes charged with the contents of the unconscious which allows the firewater to obtain a collective destructive potential. This leaves what little awareness is left possessed in a cycle of addiction. The difficulty of breaking the influence of the spirit of alcohol within the traditional framework is exemplified by the following quote obtained by Raymond:

> The physical representative of the spirit enters through the mouth and circulates through the body. The object is not animate until it enters the body. It becomes animate and diffuses itself throughout the person so that it cannot be extricated by the blowing and sucking methods of the shaman. It makes the individual desire its presence. He objects to its removal. He desires the company of others who have the same object within them. Its presence is used to explain and excuse the loss of control and crazy behavior oftimes exhibited by the individual.
>
> Spirit intrusion occurs when the thought of alcohol in the body attracts its master to the mind. It is an evil spirit that attempts to invade the mind. The spirit strengthens the bad side of the individual and attempts to envelop the soul. It seeks total possession and obedience of the individual to its power. It attempts to control the mind and fill the soul with negative sacred power. (Raymond 1983, p. 61)

The complete domination by the alcohol is apparent; this domination is easily apparent to those who have been in the grasp of this devastating force.

Most of the methods that we have used with people suffering from alcohol addiction was invented as the situation required because nothing else was working. We welcomed the whole notion of alcohol spirits and possession because we thought that this may be simply a peculiarity of how we interpreted archetypal psychology. One of the initial patients seen had been referred for testing by a local treatment center; this case exemplifies the treatment method we advocate.

As is customary, E.D. began by taking out psychological test instruments and began to administer them, since that is why he was there. No sooner had he started administering some projective tests than the patient started talking about his dreams. After going back to the task of testing, the patient would quickly bring the conversation back to his dreams. E.D. decided to go along for a while, and soon they had spent three sessions discussing the patient's dreams. Obviously dreams were important to this man. By discussing his dreams he was becoming psychologically stronger even though at this time E.D. was in the process of understanding some of the symbolic subtleties and he was not very experienced in dream interpretation.

The dream motif that emerged over and over again was one in which alcohol had a consciousness of its own as it approached him in the dreamtime. The idea that alcohol was a spirit that emerged from the bottle was vividly portrayed by the client in a drawing in which he had a demonic-looking creature emerging from a bottle. The notion of the spirit in the bottle is well described by Jung in his discussion of the *spiritus mercurius* that once released is very difficult to control (Jung 1967). Further study led E.D. to understand the dual nature of the spirit in the bottle, which can be used in a positive way such as in the Mass, representing the blood of Christ, or in a negative way as in alcoholism.

Recently the concept of the dual nature of the spirit has been further validated by traditional Native American thinking. The introductory statement by Francis Auld that opens this chapter leaves little room for speculation. The fact that alcohol is a spirit that could come back to the grandmother's "bad side" leaves little doubt about alcohol acting through the shadow side of the personality and the risks that are entailed in alcohol. Auld warns people that "the important thing is the way you let go of a bad spirit, so it does not come back on you." This notion was made apparent in clinical practice: most of E.D.'s patients in some type of treatment center reported having alcohol come and visit them in dreams or while awake.

At this point E.D. was very perplexed and had to improvise in order to continue dealing with the idea of alcohol as an entity in a way that validated the patients and made some clinical sense to him. The most obvious thing to do when spirits or entities talk to you is to ask them who they are and what they want. The direct questioning of the alcohol spirits became pivotal in the therapy because for the first time while struggling with alcoholism, these patients were no longer defenseless and were on an equal footing with the entities that were tormenting them. Another obvious intervention that emerged is the showing of respect to the forces that were involved. When the patient was struggling after a few weeks of sobriety, E.D. would suggest that perhaps the spirit could be appeased with an offering. Tradition allows for offerings to be made and is an integral part of Native American life, as we give offerings daily to the Creator and Creation.

As part of engaging the client with the spirit in the bottle, E.D. also had clients talk to the spirit of alcohol the next time that they found themselves in a situation in which alcohol was present. This was a perplexing task at first, but one of the first things that people who were trying to stay sober encounterd was an offer to drink with friends or relatives. At the point when the alcohol was actually being served, E.D. asked clients to have a conversation with the spirit in the bottle, which allowed for the psyche of the client to become aware as to the risk involved as well as to activate the unconscious process of the group that may be present whenever the conversation with alcohol takes place. We have had reports of this simple act creating a difficult environment for further drinking, and usually the client is able to withstand the temptation, since they have taken the offensive "warrior" stance as opposed to the victim stance.

The offerings and talking (talking to the alcohol can be equated to active imagination in Jungian psychology, which allows the client to engage with unconscious imagery while being aware of doing so) served a dual purpose. By beginning the dialogue and leaving offerings to the alcohol, the client was able to continue the therapy outside of the office, since therapy required that the client continue being aware of the problem even at times when s/he was not craving alcohol (this was a type of paradoxical strategy that allowed for the client to exercise his/her will in a "warrior tradition). The second benefit that the client acquired by going through these strategies was that the client started to practice traditional behaviors in a positive way. The client then became more interested in what all of this "spiritual stuff" was about; this provided an opportunity to get the patient to start a dialogue with the traditional healers.

The notion of dealing with the alcohol spirits in this manner has been both very useful and very powerful not only in working with individuals but also in working with groups of people suffering from this problem. Many Native American people have told E.D. that they have had experiences with these entities for a long time, but were not allowed or encouraged to deal with them in contemporary treatment programs—even in the ones run by IHS.

Shortly after the client becomes strong in his/her sobriety and in his/her practice of tradition or Christianity (which also allows for these metaphors to be enacted), it becomes important that the client take on a more offensive approach to his/her life. A client who was at this point in therapy told E.D. that he was afraid to walk down the alcohol aisle at the grocery store because of the possible temptation. At the same time in his life he had been seeing shadows or entities behind his curtains at home (he had about seven months of sobriety at this time). E.D. and the client identified the shadows as alcohol spirits that were starting to look for him. The way we explain this is that any time that there is a separation there has to be some sense of loss not only on the part of the client but also on the part of the alcohol—after all, they had a very intimate relationship for many years.

At this point it became necessary for the client to perform purification rituals in order to ensure that his house was free from these entities. Tradition also has prescriptions for this activity through the practice of smudging or burning strong sage in the house. Again, this keeps the client aware and in a constant warrior frame of mind versus his/her previous frame of mind of being a victim. The fear of walking through the alcohol aisle at the store also had to be dealt in a warrior stance by simply going through the aisle and asking the alcohol "What do you want?" and perhaps by leaving a tobacco offering somewhere so that those spirits are appeased.

During the initial stages of the therapy the client also needs to understand the dual nature of alcohol. An effective way of providing this understanding was given to us by a traditional teacher who viewed alcohol or drugs as being medicines, the good or evil consequences of which were entirely up to the individual. Accordingly, if one chooses to disrespect the spirit of the medicine then the spirit of the medicine will turn on them and work in a destructive way instead of a healing way. Most of the clients that have been told this agree and have no problems understanding the idea.

Some clients seen have been suffering from alcohol addiction for such a long time that it is not likely that they are going to stop drinking. These clients are on the verge of death; some of them will die within a short period of time. With these patients as with all of the addicted people treated, we try to make them aware of the options that they may have, death being one of the options. An idea from Nietzsche has been very useful in this work where at times there appears to be no hope is that there is nothing worse than suffering without meaning (Jung 1988). The idea of meaning has been all that I have been able to offer as therapy to many people. That meaning includes What does it mean that you are going to die from drinking alcohol? At times the honesty of this question serves to bring the client into awareness and helps them decide what turn their life should take.

Another notion that has been very useful in working in inpatient as well as outpatient settings is the idea of suffering. Many clients get involved in feeling sorry for themselves and in thinking that their suffering is a punishment for something that they have done. We try to explain that suffering is a sacred thing and should not be wasted. Instead, they should offer up their suffering as a sacrifice for the well-being of the people. We are not proposing that the client should be encouraged to go out and suffer on purpose, but that the suffering that they have already done and are doing should not be wasted. The image we give them is the one of the Sun Dance, where people willingly suffer for the people. This idea of suffering being useful accomplishes a change in attitude that allows the person to engage in treatment in an honest manner, since in this way suffering that may otherwise be repressed or suppressed may emerge.

Once the client has achieved a steady level of sobriety, they usually will report a feeling of isolation due to the lack of desire to go to previously attended social functions that involve the use of alcohol. The therapist should have knowledge of other places where a healthier socializing may be possible. The therapist lets the client know where there are traditional activities that maintain a strong traditional context without alcohol as well as other nonalcoholic gatherings, so that the client can began to form a different life-style. Without an integration of life-style, the therapy is in jeopardy because the temptation to drink may be constant.

Inpatient Treatment

The work that we have done in inpatient settings includes most of the methods discussed up to this point. One of the crucial differences in working with inpatient clients is that the client will be in treatment for a limited period of time. The period of time that the client is in treatment varies from 60 to 180 days depending on the program termination policy. The reduced amount of time that we have to work with such clients presents some theoretical problems when implementing analytic strategies (most analytic strategies are long-term treatment on the order of three to five years).

A method we have used to take into account the duration of treatment and still offer effective long-term intervention has been the use of a didactic teaching strategy. Most of the teaching is directed at instructing the client on how to work with his/her own unconscious material (dreams, drawings, fantasies, etc.). The teaching is done in a group therapy setting and the clients all participate in the process.

In the group, the client reports his/her dream and we write the dream on a large piece of paper in front of the clients. We then proceed to make sense of or interpret every image and action presented in the dream. The interpretation is first done by the client who has the dream, and then other clients add their feedback. Once the dream has been interpreted to the satisfaction of the dreamer, we take the large piece of paper with all the notations and give it to the dreamer in a very respectful manner.

In our experience, the method of dream groups has been very useful. Dreams provide intrapsychic insights to the client that are usually outside of his/her ability to access. The dream groups serve to accelerate the therapeutic process because most dreams are very symbolic, and resistance by the ego is thereby avoided. The lack of ego resistance to the symbols allows for painful and traumatic psychological material to emerge within the safety of the treatment process. The client is then able to work on deep psychological issues in conjunction with working on his/her problem of chemical dependency. The client usually has a realization about the reason why s/he abuses substances; this reason is usually to avoid getting in touch with the pain that underlies the addiction.

The client is empowered to continue the treatment for as long as s/he wants once s/he leaves the treatment program since the analytic tools acquired can be used outside the treatment setting. In the ideal situation, the client is to engage in ongoing therapy once s/he leaves the program. Unfortunately, long-term therapy is not a commodity that most Native American people can afford, and there are very limited resources that the client can access that will address his/her worldview in a manner that will be constructive and culturally relevant.

One of the most painful, common, and difficult problems found in working in inpatient settings is the problem of incest history. Many of the clients with whom we have worked as well as many of the reports that we receive from therapists working in Native American country substantiate the problem of incest history. The clients who are afflicted by incest history find it exceedingly difficult to remain sober while the incest trauma remains unresolved.

Incest resolution becomes more difficult when the traumatizing event is not accessible to the awareness of the client. This lack of awareness is common, and clients report having anxiety, depression, and the desire to abuse alcohol, yet do not know why they feel these symptoms. The vehicle of dreams is very useful in accessing the trauma because most of the dreams that deal with the incest will be symbolic and not easily recognizable to the client's awareness. Through the interpretation of dreams, drawings, poetry, and fantasies, the trauma can be brought to consciousness. The therapist should not bring up the incest in the process of interpreting the material and should instead allow the client to become aware of the trauma in his/her own time.

Once the client is aware of the trauma, s/he should be allowed to work on feelings of anger, guilt, and self-depreciation. By helping the patient become aware of how the trauma was causing discomfort, the therapist sees that the client begins to understand that s/hc has power over the feelings that may have required the anesthetizing quality of alcohol or chemicals. The client is then able to understand his/her alcoholism as a reaction to a violation that was perpetrated on him/her. Alcoholism can then be understood as a symptom of deeper underlying pain, and this understanding is then useful to the client whenever s/he gets the strong desire to abuse drugs in the future. By being aware of the fact that alcohol serves as a masking device for inner pain, the client can then began a process of introspection whenever the desire to drink or abuse drugs is experienced. The awareness of alcohol desire as a mask serves as a prevention device in the client's life from the time that s/he learns about resolution of deep pain.

These do not exist in a vacuum. These interventions are remarkable in working with Native American clients and are used in addition to other sound clinical therapeutic strategies such as psychodynamic therapy, family therapy, marital therapy, and dream therapy. The therapy is a process wherein one cannot predict which strategy will work today versus which one will work tomorrow. An open mind must be kept at all times. Many times in the course of the therapy we smudge the office in order to clear the place of negative entities and to role model for the client the importance of tradition as a part of daily life.

Most of the Native American clients with whom we have worked have experienced a long-term struggle with some deeply seated anger that borders on rage. The suppressed anger and rage is one reason why so many Native American people appear to be stoic and not feeling. If they were to get in touch with their feelings, the rage level might have disastrous consequences. At times the alcohol serves to mask these feelings of anger. Underneath the rage or anger is another level; this is the deepest layer and the most difficult to deal with by non-Native American therapists—namely, tremendous feelings of grief. This grief has never been allowed a chance to heal.

Grief was touched on briefly in the discussion of the soul wound. The trauma of the loss of land, culture, and people has never been resolved, but has instead been anesthetized by alcohol and other drugs. Native American people suffer from post-traumatic stress disorder as a consequence of the devastating effects of genocide perpetuated by the U.S. government. Most therapy in the area of anger and grief resolution offered to Native Americans by non-native Americans may fail. More than one client has told me that there is no way they can share their anger and grief with a white therapist, although there are Western therapists who have been sensitive enough to deal with the issue.

Sensitivity about the grief issue may be a misnomer—honesty is more appreciated and respected. The therapist needs to deal with the anger and grief in a historically accurate way, and the patient will then respect the therapist enough to be able to talk about the grief. The therapist should be careful not to fall into the trap of being an understanding liberal, because the client will lose respect for the therapist. By using liberal jargon the therapist is showing the client that s/he is in denial about his/her collective responsibility. We have white interns ask their clients who they see when they look into their eyes: Do they see Custer? Do they see a destructive white person? In this process the therapist tells the patient that it's natural to see them in a truthful manner.

The notion of honesty in therapy is not so different theoretically from any other resolution of transference, although it may be a bit more painful for the therapist. Lockhart (1981) describes historic distrust that needs to be addressed. Historic distrust and the transference that ensues starts before the client ever comes in for treatment. Most agencies are operated by federal or local government and it is with government agencies that much of the distrust has been nurtured. Therefore, by the time the client walks into the therapy session s/he has already accumulated strong feelings of distrust for the therapist. If the therapist is truthful and works to resolve the historical transference early on, then the therapy has a higher probability of being successful. The truthful exchange may be the first time the reality of the grief underlying the client's anger has been validated. To do otherwise within a healing circle is gross treachery.

As an illustration of how close to the surface the collective soul trauma is, E.D. saw a patient who was walking in an area of her reservation. The patient reported finding herself in the middle of cavalry horses and soldiers, complete with sound. When she asked some of the elders about this they told her that in that very spot a massacre had taken place before she was born. Here is a clear example of someone reliving a traumatic event though they were not there originally. We always tell patients who report this type of feeling that they were actually there as the event took place. This can be seen either symbolically or as a compression of space time in the psyche that actually allows the person to have a personal account of the event.

Another client had been struggling with anger and feelings of depression while medicating himself with alcohol. In the process of the therapy he was looking through a book in which a description of the Trail of Tears was given. As he described an old man kneeling he once again was able to see his ancestral land. The client became emotional and began to tell E.D. he didn't know why this bothered him so much since it happened a long time ago. E.D. and the client discussed the experience and arrived at the conclusion that, at least symbolically, the client was that old man and he had never dealt with the grief. This made sense to the client and he was able to use this as a bridge into the other problems that were being manifested by his constant use of alcohol.

Another client, after some extended sobriety, came in one day wondering why a movie that depicted a massacre scene had left him so angry and hurt. E.D. and the client discussed the intergenerational grief, and with this awareness of intergenerational trauma the client began the resolution of the grief. Some medicine people have equated the treatment process as one in which we not only treat the client but are also treating our ancestors, since it is only in this plane of existence that we get to accomplish resolution of life events. If we do not work out a resolution for our ancestors, we are then only ensuring that our children will be left to continue struggling with the problem.

One of the biggest questions that we have been asked and have asked ourselves is, Why did all this have to happen?

Many explanations have been offered by researchers, therapists, agencies, etc., concerning the level of devastation alcoholism has had in the Native American community. The fact that alcohol serves as a tool of domination cannot be disputed, since people who are chronically addicted to alcohol or any substance can be more easily coerced into subjugation than those who are not. If Native American people had had this high level of alcoholism during the Native American wars, history would not reflect the resistance that was given to the conquering Europeans. Presently, keeping Native American people subjugated makes it much easier for governmental and private entities to take land and resources away from Native American control. When Native American people do question the appropriateness of such behavior from these exploiters, these people are quickly brought to trial on any number of charges that are for the most part fabricated and quickly placed in federal penitentiaries.

Since alcohol has a dual nature there is a possibility that we presently do not understand the collective dynamic of which alcohol may be a part. Alcohol may also serve a spiritual purpose in that the illness that it inflicts on the individual may be an initiatory one. This notion has been brought forward by Raymond

(1983) and deserves mention. The fact that through the process of being addicted and the subsequent recovery a person undergoes extreme personal pain, injury, and sometimes actual psychological and physical dismemberment alludes to shamanic initiation. This process of suffering is one in which the shaman must partake if s/he is to become a true shaman.

The collective ramifications of this notion can be far-reaching in that a whole community has undergone dismemberment through the process of the conquest and alcoholism. Once the community as a whole has made it to recovery, the Native American community can serve as the source of further healing to other communities. Even though this notion is speculative at this time, all we have to do is see how much hunger there is currently in the white community for Native American traditional values. Many white people have realized that their individualistic worldview is not working and are looking elsewhere for a more community-oriented way of life that is more existentially and spiritually meaningful.

Conclusion

This chapter has attempted to investigate the meaning of alcohol for native peoples through historic social movements and to integrate these perspectives through traditional, theoretical and clinical frameworks.

There are probably as many ways to study alcohol-related problems for Native American people as there are Native American people with alcohol-related problems. Insofar as health education and clinical practice are applied disciplines, the efficacy of methodology and conceptual frameworks cannot be separated either from the applicability of the knowledge they produce or from the direct or indirect effects on domains of inquiry. A clue to successful research and intervention is already evident in the literature.

Alcohol research for this population must be informed by the meaning of alcohol for specific groups. The cultural, social, economic, political, and historic considerations that constitute meaning for various tribal and clan groups cannot be universalized or decontexualized without rendering them impotent as a guide for intervention. Research must take into consideration the alternative discourses employed by groups of people to understand illness, disease, and social pathology. The behavioral scientific narrative is but one story, albeit an important one, in informing prescriptions toward the amelioration of alcohol-related problems.

The research process itself has implications for the replication of social relationships that contribute to alcohol problems. This brief analysis has tried to demonstrate that many native groups have resisted the displacement of their master narratives in the understanding of illness, disease, and dysfunction. The recognition and credibility of indigenous understandings are, in part, bestowed by academic, funding, and governmental agencies. If research emanating from these arenas adheres to a strictly behavioral interpretation of social problems, its effect is displacement and disempowerment. The process of self-determination starts with the ever-evolving processes of self-identification and self-construction.

6

Intervention with Families

Their ideal is to be men; but for them, to be men is to be oppressors. This is their model of humanity. This phenomenon derives from the fact that the oppressed, at a certain moment of their existential experience, adopt an attitude of "adhesion" to the oppressor. Under these circumstances they cannot "consider" him sufficiently clearly to objectivize him—

to discover him "outside" themselves as oppressed is impaired by their submersion in the reality of oppression. At this level, their perception of themselves as opposites of the oppressor does not yet signify engagement in a struggle to overcome the contradiction; the one pole aspires not to liberation, but to identification with its opposite pole.

—Paolo Freire

Work in the Native American community requires that many of the interventions used involve the whole family. Many times family involvement is not possible due to geographic considerations, or there may be members of the family who are unwilling or unable to work on issues of importance that will contribute to the well-being of the family. Those who are not amenable to family therapy can be treated individually or referred for appropriate intervention to a traditional healer.

Unfortunately, many of the families with whom we have worked in Native American country have core issues of alcohol dependency somewhere in the family system. Chemical dependency further complicates the clinical picture because alcohol and other drugs bring with them a whole range of dynamics that need to be addressed. At times the family member must go into inpatient treatment for substance abuse before treatment of any value can occur within the family. Issues of codependency, enabling, and the usual dynamics along with historical considerations make the task a very challenging one, to say the least.

Once the therapist is aware of some of the aforementioned historical issues, s/he can begin to implement some of the available strategies available from the Western camp. Therapies involving communications, structural, and other systemic approaches can be quite effective if the therapist has knowledge and also validates some of the historical issues that have had a profound intergenerational effect on the Native American family. The validation must be done within the context of the actual therapy, so that the family becomes empowered through the realization that some of the family craziness is due to outside forces—such as the long-term oppression of Native American culture within the social milieu of occupation that persists to this day.

In our experience, once the validation of the externally imposed craziness is accomplished, the family system is very amenable to intervention. Apparently the catharsis provided by the acknowledgment of the historical factors allows for an atmosphere of honesty to emerge. Within this honest vessel the family is able to find security and the safety net required for some of the personal family pathology to be dealt with. In our work with Native American families we have found that one of the effects of the systematic disruption of the family system through the implementation of intergenerational ethnocide is a rate of child abuse which equals that of the non-native American population. The incidence of child abuse can also be traced directly to the destruction of Native American culture in which the care of children was regarded as a sacred trust.

Whenever a person or persons find it difficult to express frustration or anger due to living in an oppressive environment, the frustration or anger becomes internalized. Paolo Freire (1990) outlines the notion of internalizing the oppressor as one of the by-products of colonialism. The oppressed group, by internalizing the oppression, may have a tendency to become like the oppressor because the introjected oppression has no place for expression. The anger and oppression can also be expressed in an unhealthy manner through domestic violence.

The incidence of domestic violence within the Native American family and community has been increasing to a level that equals that of the white population. The most heartrending manifestation of this internalized destruction is when the violence is escalated to the level of homicide or suicide. An equal amount of lamentation is being heard in the Native American community due to the amount of child abuse occurring in the family system.

Practitioners, educators, and helping professionals from all disciplines are presently receiving a tremendous amount of referrals for assessment and treatment of child abuse. The abuse ranges from physical to sexual and emotional trauma, all of which are being inflicted on large proportions of Native American children. Programs that are funded through the Indian Child

Welfare Act (ICWA) are presently overworked in the area of placement, evaluation, and treatment of child abuse.

Factors such as cognitive, emotional, and social development must be considered in the diagnosis and treatment phases of child abuse. There are various methods of evaluating child abuse; these methods are not addressed here because they are already a part of the available literature (Adams and Tucker 1984; Albino 1954; Benedekt and Shetky 1985, p. 87). There will be cases when the therapist will not know with certainty if the alleged abuse is real or part of a pathological delusion in the family. The case may be compounded greatly if the family system is suffering directly or indirectly from alcoholism and/or substance abuse. In these cases there may be scapegoating, and the denial systems are difficult to work with. It is imperative to separate denial due to substance abuse from the denial that is common among perpetrators of child abuse. Many times the denial is compounded by repression, which leaves some of the important information out of the reach not only of the therapist, but also out of the reach of the victim.

Chemical abuse has a tendency to bring family functioning to a very primitive level at which reality and delusional boundaries are not well defined. The cases where repression is strong require creative approaches in order to unmask the problems. Social service systems use anatomically correct dolls in order to have the child tell the story of what happened. In cases where the child wants to please adults, this may be an invalid practice because someone in the family system may have an investment in the child accusing another member or nonmember of the family. The accusatory dynamic contaminates the assessment to a level that invalidates the process, also placing family members at risk for unjust prosecution.

Another threat to the validity of using the doll assessment is "that children viewing the unusual sight of dolls with genitals are more likely to be stimulated to invent fanciful tales of abuse" (Use of "detailed dolls" questioned, 1988). Children may also exhibit behavior that may be interpreted as child abuse, especially when the assessing person is not a sophisticated examiner (at times the assessment is performed by minimally trained social service and law enforcement personnel). The therapist needs to be sensitive to many issues when abuse is suspected and his/her own biases should be of critical concern. Expectancy bias may prove to be destructive to a family or individual who in reality is not a perpetrator of child abuse.

Assessment is a difficult task even under the best of conditions, and our science (which is actually more of an art form than science, although there are those in our ranks who themselves are in denial as to the lack of pure science in psychology) is very limited in being able to really explain and predict behavior through the use of assessment techniques. Testing and assessment are undergoing daily changes and some of the acceptable methods of the past are seen as useless by today's standards. Even though there has been much effort made in the development of assessment techniques and methodology, the available procedures have not yet proved to be adequate to the task of assessment and prediction in clinical settings. The issue of assessment takes on additional dimensions when one considers the fact that all psychological assessment procedures are culturally biased, thus leaving assessment procedures impotent at a time when a finely tuned instrument is direly needed. For this reason new methods must be implemented and assessed continuously, especially in the critical area of child abuse where so much is at stake for the child, family, and society.

In our work over the past few years in evaluating children that are part of dysfunctional family systems, the sandtray has proved extremely useful. Sandtray methods are more objective than some other common projective methods, since they are a more open ended approach. Margaret Lowenfeld (1935) invented the sandtray and explored its psychotherapeutic uses with children in 1935. Bowyer used the sandtray to conduct studies comparing clinical and nonclinical populations. The recent popularization of sandtray use has been influenced by the work of Dora Kalff, a Jungian analyst (1969). Kalff considers the sandtray an analytic technique which may or many not be used in conjunction with other analytic methods.

To the best of our knowledge, sandtray methodology used to assess or treat abused children has not been documented or empirically substantiated. As part of our work in cross-cultural settings, it became increasingly evident that a tool was needed that would provide a more open approach in difficult child abuse cases.

The sandtray itself is a square box in which there is dry or wet sand. There should be an extensive and diverse selection of toys available which are used to create a scene. The sandplay is nondirected and the only instructions given are in response to questions asked by the patient. The response is always the same, "You can make a story, or a dream or anything you want." Most children do not ask for instructions; instead they begin play spontaneously, quickly becoming absorbed in sandworld. Nonintrusiveness is the fundamental difference between sandtray and more popular methods of assessment in which demands are made for the patient to enact or engage in projecting on a stimulus which pulls for a particular type of unconscious material. As a method of analysis, some of the techniques employed by the Thematic Apperception Test (TAT) can be utilized in assessing the responses given by the child as s/he creates a world or dream in the sandtray. Questions like What is he thinking? and Where is she going? What is he feeling? Why? are examples of the type of questions that can be asked of the client as s/he plays with the objects in the sand.

By the time most abused children are referred to a psychologist, they have already undergone extensive postabuse trauma at the hands of the very system that is supposed to help them. The child has been mandated to play explicitly with dolls in order to make the prosecution's case against the alleged perpetrator easier to prove and get a conviction. If the prosecution is not seeking a conviction, it may be that the social service providers are unsure as to what decision to make as far as child custody is concerned. The worst that our system has to offer the abused child is a cross-examination from an opposing attorney, which may inflict trauma that is as harmful as the original abuse.

There are different viewpoints from which to explain repression and how to best bring traumatic contents into awareness. As mentioned above, by the time that the child or family is seen for evaluation, most of the sociohistorical evaluations made have been for legal purposes. The children are referred to a therapist either to substantiate findings or to provide treatment or further recommendations. There is no need to further traumatize the child by using intrusive techniques. Since the abuse may be repressed and at a nonverbal level, nonverbal methods may be more appropriate as the assessment proceeds. Mood can literally act as a gatekeeper of emotional contents as they appear in awareness. Clark and Teasdale concluded that "mood has two separate effects: It influences the selection of emotional material for entry into consciousness and it also affects how pleasing or upsetting that material will be once it has entered consciousness" (1982, p. 90). The notion of manipulating a child's moods in order to retrieve painful material for any purpose is a questionable practice, especially when we consider the extent of some of the injuries incurred by children and the repercussions of bringing them into awareness when the child is not ready to reexperience the painful memory. In reality, the child will not ever be truly ready to reexperience the painful trauma memories, and the therapist needs to weigh the child's pain against the therapeutic or assessment need to retrieve repressed contents.

Some theories of repression postulated by Cheek (1989) indicate that the reticular activating system (RAS) within the brain may have the task of deciding which information is suppressed and which information is relayed to a higher nervous system (cortex) where there is more verbal access to these contents. The RAS is an area having to do with physiological directives concerning survival and it is where higher centers can be checked against pain (both psychological and/or physical). Cheek has also done extensive work on nonverbal processes (1989), which are accessible through ideomotor responses (responses that are accessible by muscular movement while under hypnosis). Through ideomotor hypnotic techniques, Cheek has been able to access repressed and suppressed traumatic memories that are otherwise concealed from awareness and has accomplished this without further traumatizing the patient. By being able to access this non-verbal level of psychological process, a clinical application is available to address some of the repressed material found in cases of child trauma.

When the child is allowed to express him/herself in a non-verbal manner, it is possible that traumatic events will be revealed in a nontraumatic, symbolic fashion. Because many children neither have a large verbal capacity nor consciously realize that events may have been traumatic, it is reasonable to use methods that may release repressed material in a more symbolic, nonverbal way. The sandtray provides the child with a nonverbal vehicle that allows for symbolic ideomotor responses that have cathartic and therapeutic qualities. The sandtray is also pragmatic because the therapist does not predispose the child to give any particular type of response, as is the case in many other assessment procedures.

The child, without being aware of the meaning of his/her play, can symbolically play out the theme of the abuse and at the same time begin a healthy reconstruction of the trauma through therapeutic intervention that is concurrent with the assessment process. The symbolic play is even more important in cross-cultural work, where cultural norms may neither be conducive to excessive verbal activity nor accessible to orthodox psychological assessment methodology. During the symbolic reenactment the child can begin to resolve the trauma at the same psychological level at which the trauma occurred, i.e., through ideomotor memory. The story is being told by the physical body with little or no involvement on the part of the cortex processing centers. By symbolic resolution, the child is not forced into awareness before s/he is ready and the psyche of the child is protected. Repression, after all, is occurring for a purpose—that is, for the preservation of the totality of the personality, which may be vulnerable to some of the images and memories of the trauma.

By making the child relive the traumatic experience at a conscious level of awareness before s/he is ready, we are not respecting the survival quality of repression and run the risk of further disintegration of the personality. If the child has not suffered a trauma such as sexual molestation, then we also preserve our objectivity by simply allowing the child to express what s/he enacts in a free play situation, without biasing the assessment through expectation.

The child, through symbolic play, can work through some of the trauma in a method that is not intrusive and gives the child all of the control in the process. This is important because a therapist who moves too fast may harm a child who does not have the ego strength to cope with the issues in question. A sensitive therapist uses the sandtray very much in the way that dreams are used to cue when the personality is ready to move forward in the treatment of a specific complex. The child can also rearrange the world in the sand from a pathological one to a healthier one, which is critical in treating children who have been hurt. Through sandplay the child starts to rebuild trust, and if the family is also involved in the treatment, then the process can be a healing one for the family system.

The prime concern in the assessment process should be that of preserving the integrity of the child's psyche. Much of the material desired by the judicial system can be accessed most of the time without further trauma. Sometimes the data revealed by sandtray assessment contradicts some of the findings of social services assessments. In such a case, extreme care should be taken not to nullify the child's previous testimony while at the same time trying to ensure that an alleged perpetrator is not unjustly convicted. There is no fail-safe system, and the ability for psychology to be completely sure of its findings are in the distant future at best.

The therapist should observe the play of the child with minimum interference, especially in the beginning. This is to safeguard against the thematic/symbolic play paralleling the wishes of the system. The toys should be arranged at random so that the child is not influenced by the structure of the arrangement. The therapist should ensure that the child has toys which are easily recognized in a cross-cultural context. Cross-cultural stimuli are not available in the Thematic Apperception Test or the Children's Apperception Test and are of critical importance when assessing Native American children (or other nonwhite children).

Most of the play that the child presents is self-explanatory, and most therapists have no difficulty in identifying the thematic content of the worlds that the child creates. The following are some guidelines that generalize across situations, although each world that the child creates has its own unique quality and meaning for that child at that particular stage of development.

In most of the sandtray worlds there is a main protagonist. The theme has a main character or situation, whether depicted in human form as in the Thematic Apperception Test or animal form as in the Children's Apperception Test. The therapist should follow this part of the story with obvious interest, and toward the end of the child's play, if an inquiry seems in order, then inquiry should be done as unobtrusively as possible.

The sandtray world also has a symbolic character who is the recipient of the action. Again, the obvious needs to be observed (i.e., is the person/situation receiving hostility, aggression, caring, etc.). At times the child may choose to bury the figures of his/her world in the sand. Interpretation depends on how deeply they are buried. Burial may indicate the depth of repression. There have been times when the child buries the figures completely, indicating that the psychological contents are in complete obscurity to awareness. Partial burying of figures may be interpreted as psychological contents that are not completely repressed and may actually be surfacing to awareness.

Where the child places a toy in the sandtray is useful clinical information. Some obvious notions from the Draw-a-Person Test can apply to this situation. If the child stays on one side or another or if it's a large world, then the obvious interpretation may be made. More traditional Jungian interpretation of sides are indicative of consciousness or unconsciousness (left or right side of the tray, respectively). If the child is amenable to talking, questions may be asked about the world while s/he creates it.

Thematic construction is some of the most useful material obtainable through sandtray Because the themes are interpreted as the actual projections of the interactions in which the child lives in from day to day. If the child has no theme or poor quality of thematic material, this is indicative of a very poor ego reality, and the therapist should deal with the theme as in any other situation when this material is present. If the theme is well organized then the reality testing may be more intact, but care should be given in this interpretation as well. Phenomenological reduction methods should be implemented so as to keep reducing the themes to their lowest common denominator.

Case Examples

A twelve-year-old girl was referred for assessment and treatment by social services. The presenting problem was to ascertain to what extent the girl had been sexually abused. By the time that E.D. saw her, the social service system had conducted the usual study and had determined through the use of doll play that the child had indeed been the victim of sexual abuse at the hands of an older male from her extended family.

Some of the manifestations of her repressed anger were not unusual. Her family reported her inability to concentrate in school and she had regressed to wetting her pants from time to time. She also began to act in a hostile manner with some of her classmates, and her hostility was being manifested in overt physical aggression.

During the initial two sessions the young girl was very quiet, and her silence was respected. The only activity in which she participated was the nonverbal activity of playing in the sandtray. Play was initiated by her and no attempt was made to interfere or to ask questions at this point. The most remarkable event during her initial sandplay was the excessive use of toys. She used more items than had been customary for other patients who had used sandplay as part of the therapeutic process also involving talk therapy. The initial sandworld also had the quality of not having any symmetry, and the thematic content was very undifferentiated.

By the time the third session arrived the parents reported that the child was beginning to do better in school and was not acting hostile toward her classmates. She also had ceased to wet her pants, and the family was very pleased with the therapy. At this point E.D. was confused because he had had very little verbal communication with the girl. After giving her sandplay process some careful thought, E.D. realized that the girl had been talking quite a bit, except that her talking was not verbal, as we are so accustomed to hearing. The fact that she used so many of the toys appeared to be a cathartic exercise as is customary for so many patients in the initial sessions of therapy. At this point she was not ready to talk to a male therapist. Because of the sandtray she did not have to talk to E.D. while still working on her trauma and pain.

During the subsequent three or four sessions, she began to use fewer items and a very distinct symmetry and thematic content began to emerge. The thematic content included ideas of people being in danger, and the danger was usually from a male figure who would be hiding behind some sort of a wall. At this point in the treatment she also began to relate to the examiner verbally, although at this time E.D. resisted asking any in-depth questions as to the actual injury that she had received.

Once a therapeutic alliance was established, questions were asked which are similar to ones asked while administering the Thematic Appercephon Test. Some of these questions were not appreciated by the child and she would react with anger, although she did not know how to express it. At this point steps were taken to help her in expressing anger, and she was reassured that this could be done in a positive manner and that she would not be hurt simply for her expression of anger. The family was encouraged to communicate feelings so as to learn about feelings in an honest way. In this way the family was engaged in active participation in the treatment, which would extend the therapeutic process outside of the session and allow the child to grow in a fashion not wholly dependent on the therapist.

The therapy progressed to the point at which the child was able to relate symbolic themes that paralleled her own injury. At this point she was still resistant to clinical probing of how the figures felt and what they were going to do next. The treatment was still providing a container for her to be able to express anger and to become acquainted with other feelings. One of the most remarkable themes in her sandplay emerged on the twelfth session. This little patient built a hill with many figures on top of the hill. One of the most striking figures on top of the hill was an empty fifty-caliber shell which was not part of the sandtray selection and which she actually took from the window where it served as decoration. When asked what the hill was, she replied, "a volcano." The obvious thematic content of this idea was that she was still very volatile, and when asked about a possible eruption, she assured E.D. that the volcano was not going to be active.

Toward the end of the therapy she constructed scenes which incorporated male figures that were threatening the female figures, but the male figures were always behind obstacles or not presenting immediate danger. The obvious interpretation was that her awareness of the issues was more in her consciousness than it had been before, but it posed no psychological danger as long as the boundaries remained in the therapeutic container. It was not long after this that she was able to talk freely about the injuries which she had sustained from the perpetrator. The remarkable thing about her verbalization of the injuries was that her verbal discussion was not accompanied by any evidence of unusual discomfort, as is often the case in such instances. The clinical interpretation of the lack of discord is that there had been some resolution of the problem and it no longer held the same psychological charge that it once had. Therapy ended shortly thereafter; by this time, she had established a warm and friendly relationship with E.D. This positive relationship also signified some resolution concerning her transference to male figures. There have been many cases in which the same dynamics have been played out as the therapy evolves out of the sandtray.

The sandtray can also be very effectively used in conjunction with the Children's Apperception Test (CAT). One young patient was referred by social services because of alleged sexual abuse. When the child was asked about the incident, he began to compensate and to show a tremendous breakthrough of affect. E.D. ceased to ask questions and assured the child that he did not have to talk about it that day, and the mother was also instructed not to bring up the topic. The child proceeded to work in the sandtray and his initial worlds were without form and very chaotic (and a more than usual amount of toys were used). The therapy continued in this manner for a few weeks, until the child was able to recount the trauma without much difficulty. In order to prepare court testimony, the child was administered the CAT, which substantiated the findings of the sandtray. The CAT demonstrated that the child's psyche was very vulnerable and that there had been a deep trauma of a sexual nature. In this instance the projective methods used after sandtray therapy were useful in protecting the child from further trauma and also to acquire the necessary information. If the child would have merely been administered the CAT in the beginning, chances are that further trauma would have occurred because he was not yet ready to get in touch with the pain.

Family Therapy with the Sandtray

The vehicle of sand has also been very valuable in our work with families, especially where communications have not existed between fathers and sons. A family came in to see E.D. because their ten-year-old son was playing with matches and acting out by being disobedient. When they came in, the mother led most of the session and the boy merely sat and smiled appropriately, while the father did not do much of anything and did not seem to be very interested in the whole idea of therapy.

After ten minutes of this, E.D. noticed that the child was staring at the sandtray toys with a desire to play; E.D. simply gave him permission to go ahead and play. The father was sitting close to the sandtray and started to watch the boy play, and in about five minutes the father started helping the boy build a world. E.D. watched and continued to talk to the mother and to make observations about the father and son playing. They soon disclosed that the father did not play much with the boy because he was so heavily involved in daily work. By this point the father had become aware as to the cooperative effort that he and his son had just achieved and began to disclose some of his feelings within the family system. The therapy proceeded in a usual way from this point on, the important difference being that the sandtray was a tool that moved the therapy quickly into the problem of father and son and their inability to work together. The motifs that their world incorporated also illustrated the problem of the son feeling isolated from the father, and the father quickly realized the situation better than if E.D. had taken hours of talk to help him learn about the relationship.

Sandtray Used as an Ego Boundary

At times E.D. has treated patients who have been in such psychological crisis that their ego boundaries have been very uncertain. Uncertain or loose ego boundaries refer to the fact that a patient may be about to experience a situational psychotic episode (brief reactive psychosis) and there are no other resources available to the patient. On several occasions E.D. has utilized the sandtray as a transitional object for the patient as s/he leaves to go home. The patient is asked to place an object in the center of the sandtray and then to place a circle around the object. The patient is then told that the sandtray will remain undisturbed until E.D. hears from them again.

The intervention described above allows the patient to maintain psychological contact with the therapeutic situation. The patients have reported that just the fact that they knew that the sandtray had their projection on it was a great help in the crisis situation. In this way, the intervention literally provided a boundary for the psyche.

Treatment of Individuals

The discussion up to this point may lead the reader to believe that the only form of therapy being done in Native American country is related to alcohol or child abuse. Nothing could be further from the truth; the reason that we have spent such a large amount of time on those topics is simply because they are the most difficult to deal with and the naive therapist may need to spend time thinking about the strategies to be used. Many of the clients that we have treated seek therapy for the same reason that a lot of non-native American people do—simply to gain self-understanding and create a better life for themselves and for their families.

Even though these clients may simply want to individuate, the notions discussed in the first few chapters of this book still hold true. The particular type of therapy that is implemented must take into account the fact that the client is from a non-Western worldview and cosmology because most Native American people maintain some contact with tradition. This contact can be through the influence of relatives or other community associations. The therapy should be directed at allowing the client to experience that s/he is in harmony with the world. The therapist should always have traditional options available to the client if so needed. The traditional options may be simply to be aware of psychological material that is not addressed by Western psychology and to be aware of the location of traditional healers or spiritual leaders in case a referral needs to be made. More than once we have referred clients to a sweat lodge or consulted with a traditional person as to the tribal significance of dreams and other projective material that has emerged from the psyche of clients.

Treatment Strategies with Native American Vietnam Veterans

Since the Vietnam War there has been an added trauma to the psyche of Native American veterans and their families. The effect of this additional trauma is an issue that must be addressed in the therapeutic context. In the past very little help has been provided by the Veterans Administration, and most of the help provided has been through the administration of anesthetics for the psychological pain. We would be remiss if a section on the post-Vietnam trauma was not included in this book because our experience has shown that many of the families dealing with domestic violence issues are also battling Vietnam-era PTSD.

The dynamics of working with Vietnam veterans are complex in general and are very different when Native American veterans are involved. Research indicates that one-fourth of Vietnam Veterans are suffering from PTSD (Kulka et al. 1990). The reasons for this are the uncertainty of combat, little time to adapt to civilian life, and lack of acceptance by the community once they returned (Kulka et al. 1990; Ochberg 1988). Native

Americans were participants in that war, and many of the dynamics discussed in this book were the reason. Therefore, Native American Vietnam veterans are confronted with both intergenerational and Vietnam PTSD. The legacy that this leaves for the coming generations is obvious. The families of these Native American Vietnam veterans will in essence carry PTSD to the third and fourth power and the effects and symptomatology will likewise be exponential in magnitude.

The treatment of these Native American Vietnam veterans must be through therapy based on the insights provided by traditional healing. Some of the issues of treating PTSD in a programmatic fashion have surfaced in the prior discussion. The following therapeutic issues must be a part of the therapeutic honesty, and the therapist must be able to deal with them honestly if any healing is to occur pertaining specifically to Vietnam veterans who are Native Americans:

1. The Native American Vietnam veteran was sent to fight in a war for the benefit of the colonizer, who has continuously treated him/her and other Native American people with disdain and with ongoing genocide and ethnocide.

2. The people that Vietnam veterans were fighting were also indigenous peoples, many of whom maintained tribal customs and had very little assimilation into Western culture. Therefore, the Native American Vietnam veteran was not only fighting for the colonizer, he was also charged with killing close cultural relatives who were fighting the onslaught of colonialism.

3. In working with the dreams of some of these Vietnam veterans, E.D. has found that the common theme in the dream material is that the Vietnam veteran is surrounded by some of the people that he offended, and for years the dream motif repeats itself. The Vietnam veteran usually finds relief from the images through self-medication (i.e., alcohol, illicit substances, and licit substances provided through Veterans Administration Western psychiatry). The result is that the Vietnam veteran finds little or no long-term relief and many opt for a final anesthesia through suicide.

4. Spiritual leaders and clinical work done by E.D. with other clinicians from Asian traditions have yielded similar metaphors that pertain to the treatment process. During the time that people were being killed in Vietnam, apparently the traditional leaders of those communities were praying and performing ceremonies that caused the disembodied spirits to cling on to the Vietnam veterans who were guilty of the genocide. Once the Native American Vietnam veteran understands this, the treatment can then progress to rectify the situation of possession by the spirits. In the therapeutic process the requirement is for conscious awareness of this; this is facilitated through dream interpretation. The Vietnam veteran can then connect with the people in the dreams and converse with them and work out a solution at a spiritual level.

At this point the traditional spiritual leaders must become involved in the therapy, since the person must be treated as a system of mind, body, and spirit. Medicine people can then perform ceremonies, such as purification, which will help in ridding the person of the spirits that have tormented him/her for so long. The Vietnam veteran may also want to make amends to the people against whom s/he committed genocide through some work that s/he may feel is important to offer that community. It's only through this type of honesty that the Vietnam veteran can at long last find resolution for his/her personal part of the war, and the country as a collective will have to deal with the bigger issue.

Once the Native American Vietnam veteran has dealt with the spiritual forces that have tortured him/her over the years, it is time to rejoin the community at home. At long last the Vietnam veterans can have a ceremony that welcomes them into the community as true warriors who have dealt with the responsibility of fighting against other native peoples for the colonizers.

7

The Problem of Suicide

The problem with you is that you think you have time.

— Don Juan, A Yaqui Sorcerer

Literature Dealing with Native American Suicide

Most of the literature written about Native American suicide is written by non-native Americans, and the lack of understanding of Native American cosmology is reflected in the results and the methodologies these researchers employ. The methods of research are full of Western ideology and presuppositions, and these researchers continue offensive and ineffective writing about the topic simply to publish. According to Ryan and Spence, "research methodology and instruments used have not always fit in with the Native American culture studied" (1978, p. 17) Perhaps some of these people mean well, but in no other instance is ignorance an appropriate excuse. Deloria is correct in observing that an "anthropologist comes out to Native American reservations to make observations. During the winter these observations will become books by which future anthropologist will be trained, so that they can come out to the reservation years from now and verify the observations they have studied" (1969, p. 84). The study becomes the end in itself, and few of these researchers know or care about the actual issue.

The gross oversimplification and cultural hegemony is obvious to all except to some of the critical thinkers who are working in these research areas. The fact that some authors conclude that Native Americans are involved in "victim precipitated homicide" is an example of authors not getting out of the safe research vacuum in which most research is done. If these scientists were to examine the sociohistorical issues as well as the present oppression, they would perhaps cease their victim-blaming attitude that is overflowing with overtones of scientific narcissism and white supremacy.

It is incredible to us that the National Institute of Mental Health (NIMH), in a handbook for Native Americans, engaged in blaming the fundamental structure of Native American culture without any regard for history:

> Suicide and homicide are among the leading causes of death, especially in the younger age groups. Such deaths occur needlessly and are usually predictable and preventable. These same prominent causes of death affect the Native American population with astonishing frequency, although there are other fatal disorders that distinguish Native Americans from non-native Americans in the early

years of life. . . . They [the deaths] occur largely because of inadequate parental supervision, diets, and health care. (NIMH 1973, p. 1)

The authors of this document, who were working for the very government that has been at the roots of many of the problems faced by the Native American community, found it easy to blame the victim for not having healthy diets, care, and parenting. Somehow the researchers never thought about the mission and boarding school era, as they were blaming not only the family but the culture itself. Are they insinuating that Native Americans brought this on through some defective cultural factor?

The loss of culture—or, rather, the destruction of the culture—is one factor that seems to have an effect on the suicide statistics. In a recent handbook printed by IHS, Villanueva observes:

The more recent literature shows both the suicidal adult and the suicidal adolescent as holding rapidly eroding tribal tradition; the developmental social structure which for centuries established roles and expectation and guided both through the life span is tottering—for many Native Americans it is no longer applicable, for others it is non-existent. For those pueblos, tribes and individual Native American families in cities for which their traditions are viable and workable, the suicide rates are the lowest. In other words if the culture would have remained intact, we would not be experiencing the devastating problems that we are facing. The responsibility should be place in the right place and some honesty shed on the issue and then perhaps we could begin to ameliorate the problem. (1989, p. 30)

This is not to insinuate that all of the available literature is bad or not of any practical value. However, the reader should keep in mind when reading such literature that a critical-thinking approach should be taken. Literature should be read under a sociohistorical light, rather than in the darkness of blind acceptance.

Dealing with Suicide

One of the temptations for most health professionals and researchers when writing about treatment or intervention is to discuss the issue in a very idealistic fashion. This is not meant to say that what they have to offer is of no value, but realistically most of these interventions are not practical due to the nature— or lack—of resources in Native American country. By resources we mean availability of professional mental health providers, inpatient mental health beds that are affordable, transportation, and other systemic support systems that are available within non-native American, local, and/or federal government agencies.

Realistically, most of the first contact with the suicidal individual is going to be made by a community health representative (CHR), nurse, physician, friend, family member, or some other nonspecialized provider. These first contacts are critical, and if common sense is tempered with some knowledge, then the probability of suicide prevention is increased, which is the most important aspect to the issue. Many times the first contact will be all that is available to the individual; even if a hospital or professional is close by, their use may still be unproductive if those resources do not have sensitivity for the Native American way of life.

Suicide has not always carried the stigma that it presently has within the traditional community. There were ways in which an individual could cross over if s/he had decided to end his/her life. The approach to suicide varied from tribe to tribe, and it is best to consult with traditional healers in order to become better versed in the area of suicide in a traditional context. Suicide in most cases today is a reaction to the loss of balance and harmony by the individual in question. Suicide can also be explained by the notion of internalized oppression.

Usually the person who is about to commit suicide is very depressed and has lost the ability to live within the seventh sacred direction. The person's relationship with the sacred is nonexistent, and suicide serves a purpose similar to that of alcoholism. When seen in light of the "hole" mentioned in chapter 4, it is reasonable to assume that suicide may provide the balance to the spiritual side of the directions. By committing suicide the individual can experience the delusion that s/he is finding the center of the six cardinal points, while in reality s/he is merely going further out of balance by literally going into the hole that balances the sensation and intuition function. As mentioned previously, the Earth is what gives the intuition and sensation the quality of being one with the Earth. By committing suicide the person becomes one with the Earth solely in a physical way, since the Earth will take back the physical body. The separation remains within the person's spirit because the balance can be achieved only through a relationship of body and spirit. In order to achieve balance, harmony must be achieved in a plane of life within the Earth body. The balance can only be accomplished through living life as prescribed in traditional lifestyle, thus allowing for a relationship of sacred and profane levels of exist-ence. Once the balance is achieved the natural transformation will take place as a natural death occurs.

One of the methods we have used as part of treating suicidal clients is to talk about suicide and death in a symbolic way. After all, what really happens when one dies is a question with which we must all deal. Death is merely a complete transformation of the person into another realm or place. When a person wants to die it is usually because life has become too painful, difficult, confusing, and full of discord with creation. By dying, then, all awareness will change into something that we really do not know much about, but if the pain is great enough then the risk seems worth it.

At this point in the session with the very depressed person, the therapist generally finds that very little of what s/he says has any effect. Since words or content are of little use, it is helpful to talk in images or to focus the therapy in a more process-oriented fashion. Because images carry a peculiar power of their own, the quality of transcending awareness is useful to circumvent the ego defenses and address the unconscious or the heart of the matter. E.D. usually tells people that they are like a grain of corn and that in order to have a new life they must undergo similar transformation as a corn seed which has to die, be buried, and then be reborn as a new corn plant. Once the seed is put into the ground and watered, a brand new corn plant will emerge giving new life. By talking in images the therapist is literally planting seeds in the unconscious of the client so that s/he can come up with his/her own healing images that will emerge spontaneously through dreams, art, poetry, etc. The client also benefits from discussing the center of the six cardinal points and the importance of achieving centering within a life context versus ending life before they have accomplished this task.

When E.D. talks to suicidal people about their pain, they all have a common theme: "I do not want to hurt anymore." At this point, as a therapist, E.D. tells them that in order to stop hurting they should have a complete transformation, but they can do this and remain alive (much in the same way as the corn, since the corn transforms itself and stays in this realm with us). Next, E.D. goes a step further and tells them that through the process of therapy he can help them achieve the transforming event that they need and their life can change. At this point he proceeds to establish a contract with the client stating that they will work together toward the common goal of letting the client have a symbolic or psychological death and rebirth.

By engaging with traditional practices the client can begin to make sense of his/her pain and realize that it has a purpose and lessons may be learned from it. It is not enough to tell the client that all will be fine once s/he has achieved a transforming process. The client must realize that the very essence of being alive involves some type of suffering, and through traditional practices the client can begin to make sense of the suffering and the lessons which must be learned through the suffering process.

This process may take some time and is accomplished by having the person remember his/her dreams and bring the dreams to the sessions. Through dreams, the inner healing power that we all carry with us will provide the transforming images that the individual needs in order to allow for the psychological death and rebirth to occur. The person may have a series of death dreams in which s/he sees himself/herself or other people close to him/her die; these dreams will have to be dealt with by someone who is trained in working with this material, such as a therapist or traditional healer. Through the dream process the person is also connected to a strata of the psyche that is closer to the Earth intuition mentioned earlier, and the Earth relationship will help provide balance for the person.

There have been many times when E.D. has worked with people who are in the process of grieving the death of a loved one from suicide or other causes. Some of these clients have been in the grieving process for up to four or five years without being able to let go. There are certain ways to deal with grief from both traditional and Christian points of view. One of the key points when dealing with grief is that one must remain objective and respect the worldview of the person with whom one is working. If the person is a traditionalist or Christian and the therapist is one or the other or both, s/he must be sensitive and respectful to the spiritual understanding of the client. The worst thing a therapist can do is tell someone that his/her spiritual ways are wrong. In order to be a centered therapist, it is imperative to acquaint oneself with as many spiritual ways as possible to understand the client's spiritual perspective. We are not implying that the therapist become versed in all spiritual traditions, but that the therapist should at least acquaint him/herself with some underlying root metaphors found in most spiritual belief systems.

A key issue in our work with grief has been in helping the person suffering from grief to understand that his/her attachment to the deceased person is also holding the deceased in a state of suspension. The task becomes very important to the client because s/he also wants to release his/her loved one to have resolution and can only do this by allowing him/herself to go on with life. There are as many traditional interventions for grief as there are tribes, and it may be necessary to refer people to elders or spiritual leaders when they need to deal with these issues.

Most of the interventions that address grief have to do with ceremony and ritual. As is often the case, the therapist will be the only person available to do some intervention. Even though s/he may not be a spiritual leader or medicine person, s/he may have to facilitate some talk about grief until the person can meet with a spiritual leader or therapist who is sensitive to grief work among Native American people. Our experience has been that the symbolic use of dreams is very helpful in allowing the person to release him/herself and the deceased. Sometimes the dreams speak for themselves and E.D. does not do much except listen to the dream. If the therapist is familiar with smudging, s/he may suggest to the client that s/he can smudge the house if s/he is having difficulty sleeping or else s/he can pray in the Christian fashion if that is his/her way (some clients do both).

E.D. saw a client who was not able to resolve his grief over the death of a loved one. The client's life was far from being fulfilling, and the grief had lasted several years. They worked in therapy for several months, but the therapy also was not moving beyond a certain point, and the client maintained a level of depression. At this point E.D. started mentioning that the death had to be let go and the client, of course, answered by asking, How?

All of the methods of Western psychology were not very effective in this case because this client needed some type of ritual besides those provided in therapy (such as guided imagery, behavioral strategies, etc.). E.D. told the client that what was necessary was that he go to the cemetery and actually say good-bye and release the loved one. The client felt unable to do this and reported that he was not ready for this type of intervention. E.D. happened to have some medicine roots that someone had given him, and the intuition came to him to give the client some of the roots and have him hold the root when he did decide to go and have the good-bye ritual. That afternoon E.D. received a call from the client and the first thing that he said was, "What was in that medicine?" Of course, E.D. was worried that something unforeseen had happened. Upon inquiry, E.D. found that the client had gone and performed the ritual and felt fine. Shortly after that the client terminated and upon follow-up was doing well. The client had gained enough strength from the psychotherapeutic process to empower him to perform his own ritual in his healing process. Once the client is able to successfully perform his/her ritual, the therapist can be assured that the myth of the client is intact.

Another client was referred to E.D. because he was having some very serious suicidal ideas. He had a plan and was severely depressed. It seemed as if it was only a matter of time before he made another attempt at suicide (he had actually made some attempts already). The client was very depressed; some of the depression was reactive, and some of the depression was of unknown origin (consciously, at least). E.D. and the client discussed his life for a couple of sessions, and the client agreed to a contract of not attempting suicide for the time being. On the third session E.D. asked the client about his spirituality, since he was on such a serious death journey. He reported not really having a spiritual life or practice that made sense to him. E.D. asked if he had ever been in a sweat lodge ceremony, and he did not know much about the sweat lodge either.

E.D. introduced him to some colleagues who take care of the traditional aspects of treatment and left it up to the client to consult them or not as he chose. He went to the very next sweat ceremony, and by the next session, the client had had a complete change of attitude. E.D. explored the change in attitude to make sure that he had not decided to kill himself (since when people decide to end their life they at times seem to be relieved of the ongoing depression). The client assured E.D. that suicide was not a consideration and proceeded to work on his life problems for the next few sessions. Follow-up of three and four months found him still doing well, and when he did become depressed he dealt with the depression in more constructive ways.

The case just mentioned is not to say that all one must do is have clients participate in a sweat lodge. The case does speak to a comprehensive approach to treatment in which the best of the Western and traditional worlds can be the catalyst for change in an individual. The change that can be enacted may have long-term implications, especially when dealing with suicidal clients.

The interventions mentioned are not a panacea when dealing with suicide, but they do reflect the need for creative strategies within the therapeutic process. Therapists need to realize that therapy itself is a ritual, and that because of the nature of the problem or the belief system of the client, the ritual needs to be carried to different levels at different times. When working with Native American people it is imperative that the therapist realize that working on balance is crucial; the therapist should refer to or consult with traditionalists at all levels of intervention.

8

Community Intervention

You're either part of the solution or you're part of the problem.

—Carmichael

Community work is an integral part of delivering psychological services in Native American country. Many psycholo-

185

gists turn up their noses at the idea of community work and respond by saying that they are not social workers. The reality of the situation in Native American country is that therapeutic relevance can only be accomplished by implementing a model that encompasses the whole community. Therapists must not simply sit in a padded armchair where little or nothing is accomplished because of some phobia about being perceived as a social worker. In reality, there is a great amount of difference between a social worker and a community psychologist (the training is different, as is the whole manner of approach to and analysis of situations).

Community psychology is a notion that was born in this country in the 1960s; its ideology is not widely studied or practiced at the present time. The actual genesis of community psychology was actually community psychiatry as formulated by Frantz Fannon (1963). Fannon believed that many patients in mental hospitals in Algeria would do better if they were integrated into the family and community. The use of heavy medication as a general panacea was frowned upon by Fannon, and he started to discharge patients and treat them on an outpatient basis.

The same dehospitalization experiment was tried in the '60s in the United States, when President Kennedy provided funds to local communities in order to allow them to care for the dehospitalized patients. As with many other ideas of the 1960s era, deinstitutionalization worked until there was a change of mentality in Washington. The Reagan and Bush administrations systematically and with no regard for human suffering delivered a mortal blow to all facets of community health in the United States. The rationale for this action was illogical because Reagan and Bush believed or said they believed that the need could be filled by volunteers and through funding from the public sector. They did not ask the basic question, When does a capitalist ever invest money from which s/he will not make a handsome profit? There is no short-term monetary profit in investing in poor, disenfranchised people who are also having emotional problems. Therefore, funding for helping Native American people—and other communities in need—in the area of community mental health was all but nonexistent.

America has become a country in which only a privileged few have access to health care. We have achieved parity with only one other nation in the world when it comes to dealing with the oppressed in this area, the only other nation in the world that does not have a national health plan—South Africa. It seems as if the United States is choosing the role models that will ensure that the oppressed and poor remain so, and for the most part (proportionately) the number of poor is greater among the people of color. The policy being dictated in this country can only be seen as one of white supremacy akin to apartheid. Policy toward Native American people in this country and the governmental policy directed at the Native American community are perpetuating the conditions leading to poor health. The primary problem is a lack of available services and many if not more people are in need of services at this time than ever before. All that skeptics need do is open their eyes as they cross any major city and see the masses of human beings that are wandering homeless without any hope of ever achieving the basic human needs which should be a right—not a privilege. The lack of community resources is the problem that led to the development of Gerald Caplan's (1970) consultation strategies. This consultation model is designed to make the most use of services when there is a paucity of professionals to deal with the large number of problems. The model in no way pretends to fix all of the ills of a government policy that has forgotten the suffering masses of humanity. All that this consultation model proposes to do is to stretch resources as far as possible.

Caplan (1970) discussed four types of consultation in his construct; a short explanation of each along with its relevance in Native American country follows:

l. *Client-Centered Case Consultation.* The consultant applies specialized knowledge and skills toward a particular case. The objective in this approach is to asses the client's needs and recommend to the professional or paraprofessional requesting the consultation how the client can best be helped. For instance, if a

CHR has a client that is manifesting behavior that is not the norm for that community, they may ask a therapist or a medicine person for the best way to proceed with the case. The CHR will then implement the recommendation into his/her treatment plan and assist the client in getting the best help possible.

2. *Consultee-Centered Case Consultation.* The education of the person seeking the consultation is of key interest in this strategy. The goal of the education is to increase the level of expertise of the consultee. We have done many such seminars targeted at all levels of helpers, professionals, and groups within Native American country. The consultee may need to increase his/her awareness as to how to deal with a problem such as AIDS, and the consultation approach helps to fill in the need without having to have the so-called expert actually go into the field and deal with a case-by-case situation. It is apparent that the effort of the consultant can be quickly multiplied and the consultation may have an effect on hundreds of people within a very short time. By using this model it is also possible to make maximum use of funding because professional hours can be held to a minimum.

3. *Consultee-Centered Administrative Consultation.* This consultation approach is a similar to the one just described. The difference in consultee-centered administrative consultation is that the focus is on problems of a program and organization instead of on a particular problem encountered by clients. Program consultation is an instance in which the director of an agency may be having some difficulties with a particular facet of the program. We have several times assisted directors in dealing with lines of communication between staff members who for some reason could not get along. By retaining an outside expert the difficulty between staff members can be brought to resolution because the consultant brings a more objective view to the situation.

4. *Program-Centered Administrative Consultation.* The focus of this model is in the area of planning, administration, and development of new programs or improvement of existing ones. The consultant assesses program needs and makes appropriate recommendations. This particular modality is widely used these

days in Native American country in the development of mental health programs because they have been nonexistent (for all practical purposes) in the past. The director of an agency will call on a consultant to help in the conceptualization and implementation of the program. Unfortunately, most consultants that are brought in to perform the important task proceed with no idea as to the cultural variables to which they must adhere if the program is to have any level of success.

When developing a program within a community there are subtle as well as gross differences between urban and rural programs. There are also differences between rural as well as urban programs that are located in different parts of the country. For instance, there is a great difference between a reservation in South Dakota and a pueblo in New Mexico. The consultant needs to be aware of the process development versus content development of a program; there is no blueprint that one can follow with any given community.

Development in a rural setting where the health clinic is controlled by a board that is tribal based poses a different situation from a program in an urban setting. In a rural setting considerations as to the existence of local resources must be made, simply because there are some areas that are very isolated and most of the services will have to be initiated by the local health care unit. The amount of expertise available to rural clinics is less than for the urban ones simply because of geographical factors and lack of funding for professional services. Most of IHS funding is concerned with medical issues; this should not be very surprising since IHS is controlled at all levels by the medical establishment. This is an interesting dynamic when one considers that most of the problems that Native American people face are in the behavioral area and approximately three percent of the IHS budget is focused on these problems. The funding dynamic is open to interpretation; there seems to be an ongoing level of institutional denial especially in the area of community chemical-dependency funding strategies.

Urban Native Americans have been placed in a classic double bind by the federal government through the relocation act implemented in the 1950s. Through this act, Native Americans were taken from reservations throughout the country and placed in urban settings such as Los Angeles and San Francisco. The government then enacted a policy which stated that relocated Native American people were no longer Native Americans because they no longer resided in a reservation, thus leaving thousands of Native Americans socioeconomically stranded. The devastation of this policy is presently part of the problem that is destroying Native American people within the inner cities. The urban Native American is left isolated both from the tribe and from the white world, thus creating a profile of despair and alienation.

Urban settings are plagued with a completely different set of problems than rural settings in the delivery of mental health services. Not only are there over one hundred tribes represented in a place such as the San Francisco Bay Area, but difficulties in service delivery are further compounded by the fact that the federal government has systematically attempted to wash its hands of its responsibilities concerning the health needs of urban Native Americans. In addition, urban Native Americans are deprived of medical and social services due to some barriers that are systemic in nature. Eligibility requirements may be a barrier to treatment unless one goes to a reservation hospital. The lack of therapeutic relevance in white settings along with language and transportation difficulties may render services to urban Native Americans nonexistent.

Native American people are dealing with rapid changes in mobility, education, and family patterns. Native Americans who leave reservations must cope with a feeling of rejection. Young people find themselves in conflict with the dominant culture and traditional tribal culture. Stress often results from the conflict experienced by the young individual, and service goals should be to reintegrate previous life-styles with the modern, thus enabling the individual to live in both worlds.

As part of the final report of the American Native American Policy Review Commission, Alcohol and Drug Abuse Task Force, members compiled data which indicated some causes of the high rate of alcoholism and community mental problems among

Native Americans. The factors most frequently cited by Snake (1976) were (1) unemployment and poverty; (2) boredom, lack of alternatives, lack of recreation; (3) drinking examples set by tribal leaders, parents, and peers; (4) loss of Native American culture; (5) community apathy about alcoholism; and (8) lack of good education and vocational skills; G) no self-esteem or pride; H) family problems. The breakdown of traditional customs and values is a variable that appears to contribute to these problems.

Many of the problems in delivering mental health services to both urban and rural Native Americans are compounded by the health agencies themselves. Most of these agencies, regardless of board makeup or self-determination issues, are dominated by one person when it comes to the actual day-to-day practice within the agency. This domineering person is usually if not always a physician who is not Native American; most have no idea of how Native Americans perceive healing. Many of these physicians are experts in cultural hegemony and many of them openly defy the value of any type of traditional medicine. One high-ranking physician had the audacity to actually call traditional practices "voodoo" as he openly showed his disrespect both in his verbal and nonverbal communication on the topic. Therefore, although important, the factor of urban versus rural cannot began to be addressed until the local agency or clinic has expressed a commitment to relevant therapeutic services.

Even though service delivery is a difficult endeavor, it does not mean that it is impossible. One of the first things that has to be done is to ask the community what is important to the community and to let the board of directors know the desires of the community (the board is elected by the community). This is the first step in empowering the community to make a difference; without community support the program will not be effective. The provider must make the first order of business to work with some established leaders within the community and begin to design a program that will fit the needs of the community. The process is greatly facilitated if the leadership that becomes a part of this process is part of the traditional community. Also, by starting to design the program with the help of traditional people, the traditionalists can become an integral part of the program from the beginning.

The process of assessing the needs of the community is challenging and requires creativity on the part of the people attempting to bring change to the community. During the past few years there have been countless needs assessments performed on Native American communities by all sorts of well-meaning individuals or groups. Standard community assessment methods have not been practical nor have they been welcomed by the Native American community. The community does not welcome assessment activities because of its many decades of experience with anthropologists doing research. The research done by most of these anthropologists has usually been used to expand the academic literature and not to help the community.

As stated in *Archetypal Consultation*, E.D. had to utilize an ethnographic method that stresses the participant observer technique. Ethnographic methods involve a nonobtrusive process whereby the researcher actually becomes part of the community as opposed to obtrusive methods where the researcher is outside of the community. Because of ethnographic methods there have been some needs assessments conducted that have reflected some of the real needs in some communities.

It is our view that by accessing information available to our awareness in the needs assessment process, only half of the actual information is being gathered. To get a more complete picture of a community we must access the unconscious process of the community in a systematic fashion. The most readily accessible and culturally relevant method of investigation of the unconscious is through the vehicle of dreams.

In order to study unconscious processes in a manner that is valid, there are many methodological problems which must be overcome; the main difficulty is of a philosophical nature. To subject psychological events that are by definition unknown (since these events are unconscious) to be studied by a biased method of science full of presuppositions based on an ego complex creates methodological difficulties. The problem of bias in research is one that is difficult to overcome even when working within the natural sciences. As quantum theory postulates, merely by observing an event that event is changed. The problem becomes compounded when psychological events are to be studied, since the subject of study is also the object with which the study is being done. The subject/object problem has been wrestled with by the greatest minds in Western philosophy; it was not until Husserl actually attempted to address the investigation of human experience that any practical progress was made in the dilemma of subject also as object.

Through the method of phenomenology, Husserl (1975) laid the foundation for future research to be performed with the least amount of bias possible. The notion of the Epoche whereby the investigator "brackets" his biases or becomes aware of them is a contribution that is useful as we attempt to investigate psychological events or phenomenon. By bracketing our biases, then we are able to see what the phenomenon actually is instead of what our own projection of the phenomenon is believed to be. Phenomenology is a difficult and time-consuming discipline as compared to empirical research; therefore, few researchers employ the method.

Phenomenological data can be gathered through ethnographic methods, thus allowing for the combined method of ethnographic phenomenology to be useful in investigating communities with some objectivity. The investigation of the community can employ the interpretation of text given in answers to open-ended questions, as well as to text provided through gathering dream data. Since dreams are such an important part of life for Native American people, it is reasonable to explore dream material as part of community as well as individual assessment.

The assessment of dreams becomes especially difficult if the investigator intends to subject the material to a method of analysis such as the archetypal method, which will provide more cultural relevance than standard interpretation methods. Some of the inherent philosophical problems are addressed by Spiegelberg: "Dreams are discontinuous; they do not link up with one another; they do not allow for one continuous life history . . . all dream interpretation depends essentially on being awake. But this does not preclude the fact that phenomenologically the dream world has its rights as a part of the existence to which we must open ourselves" (1972, p. 340).

The issue of dreams and phenomenology becomes even more questionable when approached from the constructs of archetypal psychology. Spiegelberg believes that, "In fact, Jung's most characteristic conceptions, such as that of the collective unconscious, hardly lend themselves to phenomenological verification" (1972, p. 130). Still, Jung makes references to phenomenology in his theoretical constructs, and his method is also known as "synthetic hermeneutics," which implies that Jung thought that hermeneutical method was applicable to dream data. Jung believed that phenomenology should be based on symptomatology and that by the analytic method one could proceed to the complexes behind the symptoms. Thus it seems as if the phenomenological method may not be obvious in its applications but nonetheless it may be the only method that actually lends itself to this type of investigation.

In a more recent discussion by Carafides of the problems of phenomenology, the issue of dream phenomena was taken up once more. Carafides makes the following arguments concerning the phenomenological study of the unconscious:

> The investigation of the dream experiences of his patients led Jung to the formulation of his conception of a collective unconscious—surely something which lies beyond the range of phenomenology. But does it? It is no valid objection to say as Spiegelberg does that this conception of Jung's does not lend itself to phenomenological verification. For if that were an adequate objection we would have to indict any phenomenology that attempts to go beyond observable phenomena. Clearly, if this were the case we would have to indict Husserl himself, who left descriptive psychology far behind in his development to transcendental phenomenology. (1974, p. 77)

In order to test the notion of being able to get a more thorough and valid assessment of what is transpiring in a community, E.D. attempted such a needs assessment in a community.

By using the regular assessment techniques, he was able to obtain information on the needs in a Native American community; the needs were predictable. Most people in the community told E.D. that alcoholism, drug abuse, suicide, and family dysfunction were the main concerns of the community.

However, at the same time that E.D. was asking about the needs he was also asking people if they dreamed and if they would tell him some of their dreams. Soon he was inundated with dream material and his presence in this community automatically involved dream talk. E.D. took these dreams and applied phenomenological reduction methods in order to do a content analysis. He was able to reduce the dreams to approximately eight hundred themes that actually had basic meaning. The results were interesting, and he found that the problems mentioned during the conventional needs assessment were expressed in dreams only eight times. The overwhelming majority of themes were of "hostile environment or hostile world—either natural or artificial" (1990, p. 126). The hostility theme occurred in about 70 percent of the theme material, thus making a statement as to what the community psyche saw as the important issue.

E.D.'s interpretation of the results took some time to accomplish, and only after seeing many people in clinical treatment for a long time did the idea of a hostile world make sense. What is of issue is that something occurred at a very deep psychological level and had completely overwhelmed and destroyed the world for these Native American people. E.D. interpreted the dream content to say that the harmony with the world was no longer there. When viewed from the standpoint of the seventh sacred direction, it is apparent that the psyche of the community recognized the wounding of the environment, and that this awareness in turn was perceived as a wounding of the psyche. Harmony had become discord and the community's unconscious perception was that the world was unfriendly and hostile. The problems that were manifested and verbalized were merely symptoms of a deeper wound—the soul wound.

It becomes necessary when working with the Native American community for the therapist to keep in mind the issue of the

Figure 3. The model illustrated shows that the approach toward community prevention and intervention is a dynamic one in which all of the components are interrelated. (Duran 1990, p. 127)

soul wound as a collective as well as an individual phenomena. The therapy must focus not only on individual problems but also, as mentioned in chapter 4, on restoring to the whole community the harmony between the psyche and the Earth.

In order to accomplish a meaningful community intervention, it is necessary that a holistic approach be conceptualized. The holistic approach should be at the individual as well as collective level. A typical model that we have found to be practical and sensible within a traditional context is depicted in figure 3. The services exist within a community context, for the community, and by the community. The model can network with non-native American as well as with Native American agencies to make the services comprehensive and relevant. The model has shown efficacy both in rural and urban areas, even though there are many obstacles to overcome. Some of the obstacles seemingly emerge out of nowhere and the people putting together such a program should be constantly aware of emerging problems that need to be solved.

One of the main difficulties in attempting to implement such a model lies in trying to convince medical establishments within Native American agencies that there is a different way of addressing the health problems of the community. The model depicted in figure 3 is not static in that the parts can be in a constant state of change and evolution. In keeping with systemic ideology, any time that any part in the system changes then all of the system changes, in contrast to most agency situations where things struggle to maintain the status quo and change is usually met with resistance. The struggle is clearly felt by most agencies where the dominant "physician worldview" struggles to perpetuate itself. In the new model the relationship between Native American and non-native American agencies is apparent. One of the most important aspects of the model is the training and research component which is the sine qua non of ongoing growth and self-evaluation.

It is imperative that collaboration with the traditional therapists be an ongoing part of the program. In one urban program, the traditional component is a staff position with potential for growth depending on the needs for this service. Along with the traditional component it is important to also offer spiritual services from a Christian perspective as well, thus offering comprehensive therapeutic services to the community. When the Family and Child Guidance Clinic is networked with local alcohol and substance abuse programs as well as with intra-agency health services, the patient has the option to help him/herself within the systemic approach. By offering consultation services to other agencies it becomes possible for the family and child guidance clinic to implement the holistic model and to multiply its efforts as explained by the notions postulated by Caplan (1970).

Native American agencies encounter a difficult situation when most of the clinic's professional staff is white while the low-ranked staff is Native American. The staff composition is an issue that can be an obstacle in the implementation of a relevant mental health program. Although most of the grass-roots people intuitively know what is needed, most of them do not have the power of academic degrees that allow them to design and develop programs. There is at least one academician who has said publicly that he can implement a relevant community program in any Native American community better than any of the Native Americans living in that community. With prevailing attitudes like these, it is little wonder that our clients would rather go without services than seek out services from insensitive people. The fact that the power base in the clinics rest with the non-native Americans makes it very difficult to implement traditional strategies much less to hire traditionals as part of the clinic staff. (Although some model programs are doing this, most lag behind in this regard.)

Native American people in this country have a right to self-determination as spelled out in Public Law 93-638. The idea of self-determination must be allowed to flourish throughout all facets of life including the therapeutic, research, and training arenas. Self-determination is the sine qua non of having a relevant psychology and is the beginning of the process of absolution for the profession of psychology. Blauner (1969) supports the notion of complete community autonomy, which radically opens doors, thus fully allowing participation in mainstream institutions. For our profession to believe that solutions can come from anywhere but from the oppressed communities is akin to professional narcissism bordering on imperialism. This narcissistic attitude merely ensures that the current problems continue, and eventually the whole of society will suffer from such thinking. According to Apple (1971), critical pedagogy seeks emancipation—in contrast to what has been described as the "hidden curriculum" of modern-day American education that works to socialize students into conformity, obedience, and passivity, perpetuating the values of the dominant culture.

According to the thinking of Paolo Freire (1990), it is impossible for the oppressor to liberate the oppressed. In reality what happens in an ideal situation is that the oppressed, in enacting his/her liberation, will also liberate the oppressor. Thus the act of liberation is a process that has love as a basic guiding principle—something that is never mentioned in most Western psychology. Freire delineates the process by which communities can be empowered to develop their own autonomy. According to empowerment notions, our profession should learn to facilitate group praxis through listening to the communities. As Wallerstein and Bernstein state about their work at Zuni Pueblo:

> To Freire, the purpose of education should be human liberation so that learners can be subjects and actors in their own lives and in society. To promote this role, Freire proposes a dialogue approach in which everyone participates as equals and co-learners to create social knowledge. The goal of group dialogue is critical thinking by posing problems in such a way as to have participants uncover root causes of their place in society—the socioeconomic, political, cultural, and historical context of personal lives. But critical thinking continues beyond perception—toward the actions that people take to move beyond powerlessness and gain control over their lives. (1988, p. 382)

The Freirian approach is relatively simple and implementation in our agencies and communities can begin any time. The three-stage method is delineated by Wallerstein and Bernstein, and with equal partnership between the community and agencies decisions are not imposed as much as thought out critically within the partnership model. In step 1 all we have to do is listen to and understand the thematic content of the issues important to the community. Step 2 involves a participatory dialogue using a problem-posing method. Step 3 is praxis or the positive changes that people have conceptualized in the dialogue.

Most patients have multifaceted needs when they come to a health clinic. Being able to offer them many types of services within one building is the ideal situation, especially in urban settings where transportation can become an added burden. By integrating physical, dental, psychological, and spiritual services, the agency is more in line with traditional worldviews, which do not compartmentalize the person.

A great problem in making such a model work is one of funding. Government funding sources do not understand such an idea and prefer to continue funding programs that do not make sense when seen from the perspective of the community's needs. Most proposals must be written in such a manner that if funding is acquired, the services usually are not congruous with what the community really wants or needs. For funding purposes it becomes necessary to educate government and private funding sources as to what will be the most effective way to address the problems of the community. It is a very difficult task to provide relevant health care and mental health services, but the alternative is that the community remains unserved and the problems continue to worsen. Things will not get better by themselves, and ultimately it will be up to the community of Native American people to undertake and solve some of the problems. In order for the community to be able to solve some of these problems, the community must have an integral part in designing any facet of services.

9

Epilogue

It is more of a seeing than a looking. The flash of recognition is always a momentary thing—a turning of a moment in to another as in sighing. The glimpse of sparkle on a shiny surface. The smell of a place; the taste and texture of thought, the point between the breath's coming in to its end and starting its going out. A quick somethingness—it eludes the fixed gaze, leaving only an impression. These are the moments we say need "seizing" if we are to ride the wind. Something cautions us; do not go looking for clouds in the closet, you'll not find your shoes in the sky. The trick of "grabbing the wind" is a sort of personal exploration for me.

—Andy Curry

Many of the issues brought out into the light of day in this book will without a doubt bring up some questions as to what is really being said here. If this is the case perhaps what is happening is that a different type of cognition is being experienced by the reader. Our experience when we discuss some of these notions in seminars and classes is that many participants become upset over the material and at least initially develop a strong dislike for the process. After a few weeks, if the material is given a chance to become part of an open-minded experience, then the student begins to incorporate some of the notions into his/her own therapeutic work, usually with positive results. It is much easier to deal with feelings that are brought on through the reading of written material than it is to deal with a client who is angry at the lack of understanding and sensitivity, as is usually experienced by Native Americans in therapeutic encounters.

We have attempted to delineate a notion whereby the Western reader can use a Western theoretical construct in order to understand the Native American client when the meeting takes place in the clinical setting. By taking a theoretical construct and integrating Native American worldviews, it is possible to understand the Native American client's therapeutic needs in a more sensitive fashion.

Through the use of practical examples and specific problems we have used the new integrated notion as a tool to help the reader understand the practical application of the model. By discussing alcoholism, family problems, and suicidal issues, the notions of chapter 4 become useful in the day-to-day practice of therapy.

The discussion has taken the reader through questioning the notion of the Western worldview being the supreme worldview, regardless of what God may have told Adam in the Garden of Eden. Not all cosmologies subscribe to the Judeo-Christian cosmology, and to attempt to impose a foreign cosmology on people as was done by the missionary tradition is the ultimate act of disrespect for another human being's experience of humanness.

The attempt is herein made to merge differing worldviews and to bring out the best result when working therapeutically with American Native American people. The fact that Native American people have been subjected to the worse systematic Holocaust in the history of the world is reason to believe that this genocide may contribute to such a high incidence of problems within the Native American community.[1] Most of the problems encountered in therapy by Native Americans are due to the fact that most therapies are deeply entrenched in linear thinking that is foreign to the Native American client. Within the Native American worldview there is room for a deeper experience of being in the world than the one measured by the linear yardstick provided by Isaac Newton.

Much of the fault in the inability of Western therapists to address the needs of Native American people rests with educational institutions. There is not a graduate program in this country that offers a curriculum that makes sense to people of color in general. The core of subject material is deeply contaminated by an ambiance of "what is white is right and if you want to know about 'those' people then you can take a three-unit course that epitomizes the paternalistic attitude of academia." Academics then feel that they have performed their educational responsibility to third- and fourth-world peoples.

In writing or discussing any issue that relates to Native American people, it is impossible to address the issue without considering the political climate. Fourth-world people such as Aborigines in Australia, Indios in Latin America, or Palestinians

---

1. Some scholars estimate that from 50 to 100 million Native American people have been systematically exterminated in this hemisphere in the past five hundred years. This extermination continues in Central and South America; in Guatemala alone in the last decade 50,000 Native Americans have been killed. Much of the killing of Native American people today is still being supported by regimes that are puppets of the U.S. government.

in Palestine are presently suffering from systematic attempts at termination. Therefore, when we discuss Native American psychology, we must maintain an awareness of politics as they affect our community. The reader may find this distracting since most mainstream literature on psychological theory is presented in an acontextual manner.

Institutions do not exist in a vacuum and are reflective of the zeitgeist of the society in which they find themselves. For instance, a graduate department in apartheid South Africa would not have been in existence unless it had state funding; this funding is contingent on the university teaching the status quo. Tenure for professors and admission to students is based on a system that is reeking with overt institutional racism. It is easy to accuse the Union of Apartheid South Africa, but in reality the same paradigm is entrenched in the United States of America.

Psychology and psychiatry in this country like to point their fingers at how the Soviet mental health system exploited human beings who seemed not to be living within the psychological constraints of a totalitarian system. In any system where there is an unequal distribution of resources and power, systems of domination exist which act symbolically or instrumentally to reinforce that domination. The fact is that our society also uses labeling based on racist ideology in order to provide social control over people. The psychological effects of oppression are experienced throughout the world and most of our brothers and sisters within the profession of psychology hide behind the veil of ethics when it comes time to speak out against oppression.

Many Native American people remember the recent eugenics movement that was sanctioned by both psychiatry and psychology. Based on IQ testing, many women were sterilized to prevent them from having children unable to score as high as white children on racially biased tests. The veil of ethics is non-existent in the face of the gross violation of the most fundamental of rights—to continue existing as a people. Yet none of the perpetuators of eugenics has ever been brought to justice, although America—including many of these same eugenicists—was able to cast stones in the form of the Nuremberg trials in which Nazi war criminals were tried for similar crimes against humanity.

What about the crimes against humanity on this hemisphere? Thus far there has been no acknowledgment of these crimes, and the descendents of the colonists prefer to stay in denial about the Holocaust that they have perpetrated.

In order to make sense of the interventions proposed in this book, it is necessary for the provider to keep a sociohistorical context at the forefront of the work. It is also necessary to consider the ecological and mythological history of the community. Since the environment is an integral part of the psyche in the cosmology of Native American people, the work that is done with individuals or groups must acknowledge what the environment was like when the myths of the tribe initially emerged.

Because the stories and religion are some of the last remaining entities that are intact within Native American culture, it is important for the non-native American health care provider to acquire knowledge of this facet of life. Distrust for researchers and health care providers is still high in the Native American community and this must be respected by the people who attempt to work in this community. We recall a case in which a nursing student made a home visit and only the children were present. The student proceeded to ask the children about their religion and if they had any objects that were symbolic of those beliefs. The children proceeded to show her many of the family sacred objects and these objects were being examined when the parents arrived. That family's anger and distrust was greatly compounded, and events like this one continue to feed the mistrust that Native American people have for the colonial group. The student who acted in such an insensitive fashion was not only ignorant of manners, but her behavior can only be interpreted as an unconscious wish to continue exploiting Native Americans.

Recently, the area of ethnocide in which Westerners are active is the desecration of traditional Native American religion. Non-native American people who have lost their sense of spirituality have decided to replace their emptiness at the expense and desecration of Native American spiritual ways. Books by the dozen are being published by so-called overnight shamans who pretend to act as initiators of some of the most sacred mysteries that our ancestors preserved for us. Weekend shamanic workshops are commonly held throughout the country with no thought given as to how offensive these activities are to Native American people who have been entrusted with the caring for the sacred ways. A valid parallel to this disrespect would be for a person to go into St. Peter's Basilica while the pope is performing Mass and to take over the Mass without consideration or respect.

The amount of pain and discomfort that our community experiences due to the modern desecration of tradition is adding salt to the soul wound that these same disrespectful people inflicted in the first place. The conquering European has taken and raped the land and is now seeking to take and destroy the spirit of the land. The conqueror should realize that the tradition belongs to the Creator, and as Native Americans we are merely the protectors of the tradition. Spirituality cannot be stolen, and the more effort the white population expends in pretending to own Native American spirituality the deeper will the white person's emptiness and alienation from his/her own God become.

Because of mistrust there may be times when an intervention can only go so far, and then the natural or traditional health care providers in the community will have to carry the task to completion. By having the traditional healers deal with the specific Native American cultural facets of the case, the community will be empowered toward a greater degree of self-determination. Self-determination once implemented will establish traditional control for the well-being of the community within a traditional context. It is the traditional context that will allow for the balance of life to be reestablished in Native American country, as Native American people continue to find a way to walk in a world where high tech is the supreme ruler. Through walking a balanced road the modern Native American will be able to partake of high tech as well as traditional practice as we reestablish relationship with the Earth once more.

What Does the Future Hold?

There is much that remains to be done in the immediate and long-term future if we are to offer the new generation of Native

American people a better chance at balance as seen both in a traditional and Western context. The manner in which specific communities conceptualize mental problems needs to be investigated and new knowledge needs to be incorporated into diagnostic tools such as the Diagnostic and Statistical Manual. It is unreasonable to expect that a manual developed by non-native American people can possible include the life experiences of Native Americans unless a Native American worldview is taken into account in the description of the diagnostic categories.

The whole area of psychometrics is ready for some serious investigators to begin a complete overhaul. Objective and projective tests must be restandardized for the particular group for which they are being used. Even within the profession there is very little argument that tests are biased. What is needed mostly is for graduate programs to train more Native American professionals in order to develop a psychology that makes sense to the Native American community.

One of the ideas that is being considered in one urban community is that of tribalizing the community. By this we mean that the many tribes represented in that community would become part of an urban tribe that would function and provide a tribal structure to that community. The tribe would have a council of elders that would set standards of accepted behavior and norms for the community. The community would have to acquire ceremonies that would meet the needs of the community.

The urban tribe would have to develop quickly in the area of initiation ceremonies. Instead of allowing urban gangs and other unhealthy elements to initiate our youth, the urban tribal community would prescribe ceremonies that would initiate the youth. Warrior societies, peace keepers, and other traditional and new roles will have to be invented in order to fit the needs of a new tribe of indigenous people.

Future investigations or research in Native American country must abide by the ideology of self-determination. Research should be done only with the intent of acquiring new knowledge that is important to the community. New knowledge can also be used to protect the community from unscrupulous assumptions made by science. Native American researchers must begin to question the assumptions and root metaphors of empirically driven research that only serves to further perpetuate stereotypes about Native American people. The fact that research is used as a tool of domination should be at the root awareness of Native American tribal councils and academics who have a say in what is to be to researched within the community and how the research is to be implemented. Community leaders should take control of all research that is being performed in the community and no researcher should be allowed to publish results without input from the community. The fact that research has been used to reinforce the thinking of the majority group's concept makes perfect sense when the analysis shows that most of the federal funding for research has come from the very same source that still believes in the cultural termination of all Native American people. We must be critical in the way in which we allow for such activities to take place.

All new knowledge or research is not bad. The thing to keep in mind is that new knowledge of benefit to Native American people will most likely come from Native American people. The new knowledge must be derived from within the community itself, because who can care more about the community and its survival than the members of the community? We believe that we have the mental and spiritual resources to accomplish the task that is ahead of us and to heal the wound that has been inflicted on us. As we approach the year 2000, we are also arriving at the renewal of Native American traditions as the way of being in creation. As some friends of ours say "these aren't our ways, these are the Creator's ways, and we are here to live by those ways."

Ho! All our relations.

Bibliography

Abbas, L. 1982). Alcoholism among Native Americans. In *Native American substance abuse*, ed. W. Mitchell and Galletti. Tempe: Arizona State University Press.

Adams-Tucker, C. 1984. Early treatment of child incest victims. *American Journal of Psychotherapy* 38: 505–16.

Albaugh, B. J., and P. O. Anderson. 1974. Peyote in the treatment of alcoholism among American Native Americans. *American Journal of Psychiatry* 131 (11): 1247–50.

Albino, R. 1954. Defenses against aggression in the play of young children. *British Journal of Medical Psychology* 27: 61–71.

Apple, M. W. 1971. The hidden curriculum and the nature of conflict. *Interchange* 2 (4): 1–70.

Atal, Y. 1981. The call for indigenization. *International Social Science Journal* 33: 189–97.

Bach P., and P. Bornstein. 1981. A social learning rationale and suggestions for behavioral treatment with American Native American alcohol abusers. *Addictive Behaviors* 6 (1): 75–81.

Barnes, G., and J. Welte. 1986. Patterns and predictors of alcohol use among 7–12th grade students in New York State. *Journal of Studies on Alcohol* 47 (1): 53–62.

Barter, E. R., and J. T. Barter. 1974. Urban Native Americans and mental health problems. *Psychiatric Annals* 4 (11): 37–43.

Baynes K., J. Bowman, and T. McCarthy, eds. 1987. *After philosophy, end or transformation.* Cambridge, Mass.: MIT Press.

Beauvais, F., and S. LaBoueff. 1985. Drug and alcohol abuse intervention in American Native American communities. *International Journal of the Addictions* 20 (1): 139–171.

Beauvais, F., E. R. Oetting, and R. W. Edwards. 1985. Trends in drug use of Native American adolescents living on reservations. *American Journal of Drug and Alcohol Abuse* 11 (3–4): 209–29.

Bell, R. 1988. Using the concept of risk to plan drug use intervention programs. *Journal of Drug Education* 18 (2): 135–42.

Benedek, E. P., and D. H. Schetky. 1985. *Allegations of sexual abuse in custody and visitation dispputes. Emerging issues in child psychiatry and the law.* New York: Brunner/Mazel.

Benedek, E. P., and D. H. Schetky. 1987. Problems in validating allegation of sexual abuse. Part 1: Factors affecting perception and recall of events. *American Academy of Child and Adolescent Psychiatry* 26: 92–95.

Berlin, Irving. 1985. Prevention of adolescent suicide among some Native American tribes. *Adolescent Psychiatry* 12: 77–93.

Berkhofer, R. 1978. *The white man's Indian.* Vintage: New York.

Bhabha, H. 1983. The other question–The stereotype and colonial discourse. *Screen* 24: 6–23.

———. 1991. Conference presentation. In *Critical fictions,* ed. P. Mariani. Seattle: Bay Press.

Blauner, R. 1969. Internal colonialism and ghetto revolt. *Social Problems* 16 (4): 393–408.

Blum, K., S. Futterman, and P. Pascarosa. 1977. Peyote, a potential ethnopharmacological agent for alcoholism and other drug dependancies: Possible biochemical rationale. *Clinical Toxicology* 11 (4): 459–72.

Bogue, R. 1990. *Deleuze and Guattari.* London : Routledge.

Borunda, Z., and J. Shore. 1978. Neglected minority: Urban Native Americans and mental health. *International Journal of Social Psychiatry* 24 (3): 220–24.

Bowyer, A. 1959. The importance of sand in the world technique: An experiment. *British Journal of Educational Psychology* 29: 162–64.

Brachette, W. 1990. Traditionalism and the problem of cultural inauthenticity. In *Nationalist ideologies and the production of national culture,* ed. Richard Fox, pp. 112–29. American Ethnological Society, Monograph, No. 2.

Brese, P., G. Stearns, B. Bess, and L. Parker. 1986. Allegations of child sexual abuse in child custody disputes: A therapeutic assessment model. *American Journal of Orthopsychiatry* 56: 560–76.

Campbell, J. 1973. *The Hero with a Thousand Faces.* Princeton: Bollingen, 1973.

———.*The Masks of God: Primitive Mythology.* New York: Penguin, 1979.

———. 1988. *The Inner Reaches Of Outer Space.* New York: Harper and Row.

Caplan, G. 1970. *The theory and practice of mental health consultation.* New York: Basic.

Carafides, J. L. 1974. H. Spiegelberg on the phenomenology of C. G. Jung. *Journal of Phenomenological Psychology* Fall: 75–80.

Carpenter, R. A. 1981. A peer managed self-control program for reduction of alcohol consumption in high school students. *Dissertation Abstracts International* 42 (9): 3817-B.

Cheek, D. B. 1960. Removal of subconscious resistance of hypnosis using ideomotor questioning techniques. *American Journal Of Clinical Hypnosis* 3: 103–7.

———. 1962. Ideomotor questioning of subconscious pain and target organ vulnerability. American Journal Of Clinical Hypnosis 5: 30–51.

———. 1982. Considerations relative to Dr. Bernard L. Diamond's opinions on the use of hypnosis as a forensic tool. *International Journal of Investigative and Forensic Hypnosis* 5: 22–30.

———. 1989. *Clinical hypnosis.*

Clark, D. M., and Teasdale, J. D. 1982. Diurnal variation in clinical depression and accessibility of memories of positive and negative experiences. *Journal of Abnormal Psychology* 91: 87–95.

Clements, F. E. 1932. Primitive concepts in disease. *University of California Publications in Archeology and Ethnography* 32: 185–252.

Colins, S. (1987). The wild man and the Indian in early 16th century book illustration. In *Indian and europ,* ed. C. F. Fees, pp. 5–36. Aachen: Ed. Herodot, Rader Verlag.

Conrad, R. D., and M. W. Kahn. 1974. An epidemiological study of suicide and attempted suicide among the Papago Native Americans. *American Journal of Psychiatry* 13 (1): 69–72.

Curry, A. 1972. *Bringing for forms.* Paradise, Calif.: Dustbooks.

Deloria, V., Jr. 1969. *Custer died for your sins.* New York: Macmillan.

———. 1992. *God is red: A native view of religion.* Golden: North America Press.

Derrida, J. 1980. *Of grammatology.* Baltimore: Johns Hopkins University Press.

Duran, E. F. 1984. *Archetypal consultation: A service delivery model for Native Americans.* New York: Peter Lang.

Duran, E. F. 1990. *Transforming the soul wound: A theoretical and clinical approach to Native American psychology.* Berkeley: Folklore Institute.

Edmunds, D. 1983. *The Shawnee Prophet.* Lincoln: University of Nebraska Press.

Edwards, E., and M. E. Edwards. 1984. Group work practice with American Native Americans. *Social Work with Groups* 7 (3): 7–21.

Fannon, F. 1963. *The wretched of the Earth.* New York: Grove Press.

Fingarette, H. 1988. *Heavy drinking: the myth of alcoholism as a disease.* Berkeley: University of California Press.

Fisher, A. D. 1984. Alcoholism and race: The misapplication of both concepts to North American Native Americans. *Canadian Review of Sociology and Anthropology* 24 (1): 81–98.

Foucault, M. 1967. *Madness and civilization.* London: Tavistock.

———. 1973. *The birth of the clinic.* London: University of Oxford.

Foulks, E. F., and S. Katz. 1973. the mental health status of Alaskan natives. *Acta Psychiatrica Scandinavica* 49 (1): 91–96.

Fox, R. 1990. *Nationalist ideologies and the production of national cultures.* American Ethnological Society, Monograph, no. 2.

Freire, P. 1990. *Pedagogy of the oppressed.* New York: Continuum Press.

French, L., and J. Hornbuckle. 1982. Native American alcoholism. In *Native Americans and criminal justice,* ed. L. French, pp. 97110. Osmu: Totow.

Gade, E., and G. Hulburt. 1985. Personality characteristics of female American Native American Alcoholics: Implications for counseling. *Journal of Multicultural Counseling and Development* 13 (4): 170–75.

Gayton, A. H. 1930. *Yokuts-Mono chiefs and shamans.* University of California Publications in American Archeology and Ethnography, no. 24, pp. 1–420.

Gifford, E. W. 1932. *The Northfork mono.* University of California Publications in American Archeology and Ethnography, no. 31, pp. 14–65.

Gilman, S. L. 1988. Disease and representation: Images of illness from madness to AIDS. Ithaca, N.Y.: Cornell University Press.

Gould, S. J. 1981. The Mismeasure of Man. New York: W. W. Norton and Co.

Graves, T., 1973. The Navajo urban migrant and his psychological situation. *Ethos* 1 (3): 321–42.

Guillory, B. M., E. Willie, and E. F. Duran. 1988. Analysis of a community organizing case study: Alkali Lake. *Journal of Rural Community Psychology* 9 (1): 27–36.

Guha, R., and G. C. Spivak. 1988. *Selected subaltern studies.* New York: Oxford University Press.

Habermas, Jurgen. 1987. *The theory of communicative action,* Vols. 1–2: *Lifeworld and system: A critique of functionalist reason.* Boston: Beacon Press.

Handelman, D. 1976. The development of a Washo shaman. In *Native Californians: A theoretical retrospective,* ed. L. Bean and T. Blackbburn, pp. 381. Soccorro, N.M.: Ballena Press.

Harasym, S., ed. 1990. *The post colonial critic: Interviews, strategies and analysis.* Gayatri Chakravorty Spivak. New York and London: Routledge.

Harmon, A. 1989. When is an Indian not an Indian? *Journal of Ethnic Studies* 18 (2): 95–123.

Harvey, E. B., L. Gazay, and B. Samuels. 1976. Utilization of a psychiatric-social work team in an alaskan native secondary boarding school. *Journal of the American Academy of Child Psychiatry* 1 (53): 558–74.

Havighurst, R. J. 1971. The extent and significance of suicide among American Indians today. *Mental Hygiene* 55 (2): 174–77.

Hersch, J. 1980. The ethnic unconscious. The Society of Analytic Psychology 3.

Hertzbert, H. W. 1971. *The search for an American Indian identity.* New York: Syracuse University Press.

Hillman, J. 1979. *The dream and the underworld.* New York: Harper and Row.

Hodgkenson, H. L. 1990. *The demographics of American Indians: One percent of the people; fifty percent of the diversity.* Washington, D.C.: Institute for Eductional Leadership, Inc., Center for Demographic Policy.

Hoffman, M., J. Helmut, and H. Jackson. 1973. Comparison of Measured Psychopathology in Native American and Non-Native American alcoholics. *Psychological Reports* 33(3): 793–94.

Honigfeld, L. S., and D. W. Kaplan. 1987. Native American postneonatal mortality. *Pediatrics* 16 (4): 22–25.

Hulme, J. 1990. *The Enlightenment and its shadows.* New York: Routledge.

Hurlburt, G, E. Gade, and D. R. Fuqua. 1982. Intercorrelational structure of the Eysenck Personality Questionnaire with an alcoholic population. *Pychological Reports 1982* 51 (2): 515–20.

Hurlburt, G, E. Gade, and D. R. Fuqua. 1984. Personality differences between Alcoholic Anonymous members and nonmembers. *Journal of Studies on Alcohol* 45 (2): 170–71.

Husserl, E. 1975. *Ideas*. New York: Collier.

Indian Health Service. 1987. Chart Series Book. U. S. Department of Health and Human Services, Public Health Service, IHS, Office of Planning and Evaluation and Legislation, Division of Program Statistics.

Jacobs, W. R. 1972. *Dispossessing the American Indian*. New York: Scribner's.

JanMohamed, A. 1985. The economy of Manichean allegory: The function of racial difference in colonialist literature. In *Race, writing and difference*, ed. Gates, p. 83. Chicago; University of Chicago Press.

Jarvis, Boldt. 1982. Death styles among Canada's Native Americans. *Social Science and Medicine* 16 (4): 1345–52.

Jilek-Aall, L. 1978. Alcohol and the Native American-white relationship: A study of the function of Alcoholics Anonymous among Coast Salish Native Americans. *Confinia Psychiatrica* 21 (4): 195–233.

Jung, C. G. 1954. *The practice of psychotherapy*. Princeton: Bollingen.

———. 1956. *Symbols of transformation*. Princeton: Bollingen.

———. 1958. *Psychology and religion: West and east*. Princeton: Bollingen.

———. 1959. *The archetypes and the collective unconscious*. Princeton: Bollingen.

———. 1960. *The structure and dynamics of the psyche*. Princeton: Bollingen.

———. 1964. *Civilization in transition*. Princeton: Bollingen.

———. 1965. *Memories, Dreams, Reflections*, ed. Aniela Jaffe. Princeton: Bollingen.

———. 1967. *Alchemical studies*. Princeton: Bollingen.

———. 1971. *Psychological types*. Princeton: Bollingen.

———. 1988. *Nietzche's Zarathustra*, ed. James Jarrett. Princeton: Bollingen.

Kalff, D. 1969. *Das andspiel*. Vol. 1, *Handbuch der kinder psychotherapie*, ed. Gerd Bierman. Munich: Ernst Reinhardt Verlag.

Katz, P. 1979. Saulteauz-Ojibway adolescents: The adolescent process amidst a clash of cultures. *Psychiatric Journal of the University of Ottowa* 4 (4): 315–21.

Kivlahan D. R., D. Walker, D. M. Donovan, and H. Mischke. 1985. Detoxification recidivism among urban American Native American alcoholics. *American Journal of Psychiatry* 142 (12): 1467–70.

Kline, J. A., V. V. Rozynko, G. Flint, and A. C. Roberts. 1973. Personality characteristics of male Native American Alcoholic patients. *International Journal of the Addictions* 8 (4): 729–32.

Krell, R. 1990. Holocaust survivors: A clinical perspective. *Psychiatric Journal of the University of Ottawa. Revue de Psychiatrie de l'Universite d'Ottawa*, 15 (1): 18–21.

Kurtz, E. 1988. *A. A.: The story.* San Francisco: Harper and Row.

Kulka, R. A., W. E. Schlenger, J. A. Fairbank, R. L. Hough, B. K. Jordan, C. R. Marmar, and P. S. Weiss. 1990. *Trauma and the Vietnam War generation.* New York: Brunner/Mazel Publishers.

LaFromboise, T. D., and W. Rowe. 1983. Skills training for bicultural competence: Rationale and application. *Journal of Counseling Psychology* 30: 589–95.

Lash, S., and J. Freidman. 1989. *Modernity and Identity.* Cambridge, Mass.: Blackwell.

Lefley, H. 1986. Why cross-cultural traiing? In *Cross-cultural training for mental health professionals,* ed. H. Lefley and P. Pedersen, p. 90. Springfield, Ill.: Charles C. Thomas.

Leland, J. 1976. *Firewater myths, North American Indian drinking and alcohol addiction.* New Brunswick, N.J.: Rutgers Center for Alcohol Studies.

Lemert, E. M. 1954. Alcohol and the Northwest Cast Indian. *University of California Publications in Culture and Society* 2: 303–406.

Levi-Strauss, C. 1958. *Anthropologie Structurals.* Paris: Library Press.

Lockhart, B. 1981. Historic distrust and the counseling of American Indains and Alaska natives. *White Cloud Journal* 2: 31–34.

Long, K. A. 1986. Suicide intervention and prevention with Native American adolescent populations. *Issues in Mental Health Nursing* 8 (3): 247–53.

Lowenfeld, M. 1935. *Play in childhood.* London: Gollancz.

Lurie, N. 1979. The world's oldest on-going protest demonstration: North American Indian drinking patterns. In *Beliefs, behaviors and alcohol beverages: A cross-cultural survey,* ed. MacMarshall, pp. 127–45. Ann Arbor: University of Michigan.

MacAndrews, C., and R. Edgerton. 1969. *Drunken comportment: A social explanation.* Chicago: Aldine Publishing Company.

Macdonell, D. 1986. *Theories of discourse: An introduction.* Cambridge, Mass.: Blackwell.

Mason, P. G. 1990. *Deconstructing American.* Ph.D. dissertation. Department of Sociale Wetenschappen, Rijksuniversiteit, Utrecht.

May, P. 1982. Substance abuse and American Native Americans: Prevelance and susceptibility. *International Journal of the Addictions* 17 (7): 1185–1209.

———. 1986. Alcohol and drug misuse prevention programs for American Native Americans: Needs and opportunities. *Journal of Studies on Alcohol* 47 (3): 187–95.

McShane, D., and L. Plas. 1984. The cognitive functioning of American Native American children: Moving from the WISC to the WISC-R. *School Psychology Review* 13 (1): 61–73.

Morgan, Patricia. 1983. Alcohol, disinhibition, and domination: A conceptual analysis. In *Alcohol and disinhibition: Nature and meaning of the link,* ed. Room and Collins. Washington, D.C.: United States Government Printing Office.

Mosher, J. 1975. *Liquor legislation and Native Americans: History and perspective.* Working Paper F 136. Berkeley: Social Research Group, University of California.

Moskovitz, S, and R. Krell. 1990. Child survivors of the Holocaust: Psychological adaptations to survival. *Israel Journal of Psychiatry and Related Sciences* 27 (2): 81–91.

Murphy, S., and R. R. DeBlassie. 1984. Substance abuse and the Native American student. *Journal of Drug Education* 14 (4): 315–21.

Murray, D. 1991. *Forked tongues: Speech, writing and representation in Native North American text.* Bloomington: Native American University Press.

Neihardt. 1959. *Black Elk speaks.* New York: Simon and Schuster.

Ochberg, F. M. 1988. *Post-traumatic therapy and victims of violence.* New York: Brunner/Mazel Publishers.

Page, R. D., and S. Bozlee. 1982. A cross-cultural MMPI comparison of alcoholics. *Psychological reports* 50 (2): 639–46.

Pascarosa P., and S. Futterman. 1976. Ethnopsychedelic therapy for alcoholics: Observations in the peyote ritual of the Native American Church. *Journal of Psychedelic Drugs* 8 (3): 215–21.

Pelz, M. 1981. Clinical data from a psychiatric service to a group of native people. *Canadian Journal of Psychiatry* 26 (5): 345–48.

Peniston, E. G. 1978. The ego strength sale as a predictor of Ute Native American suicide. *White Cloud Journal* 1 (2) 17–19.

Perry, J. W. 1976. *Roots of renewal in myth and madness: The meaning of psychotic episodes.* San Francisco: Jossey Bass.

Peterson, K. C., M. F. Prout, and R. A. Schwarz. 1991. *Post-traumatic stress disorder: A clinician's guide.* New York and London: Plenum Press.

Query, J. 1985. Comparative admission and follow-up study of American Native American and whites in a youth chemical dependancy unit on the North Central Plains. *International Journal of the Addictions* 20 (3): 489–502.

Query, W., and J. Query. 1972. Aggressive responses to the Holzman Inkblot Technique by Native American and white alcoholics. *Journal of Cross-Cultural Psychology* 3 (4): 413–16.

Raymond, Michael. 1983. *Native American traditions: The dilemma of alcohol use among the Flathead Salish.* Masters: Unviersity of Montana.

Resnick, H. L., ed. 1988. *Erotosized repetitive hangings.* What we know about suicidal behaviour and how to treat it. London: Jason Aronson, Inc.

Rhoades, E., J. Hammond, T. Welty, A. Handler, and R. Amler. 1987. The Indian burden of illness and future health interventions. *Public Health Reports* 4 (102): 461–68.

Robbins, R. S. 1992. Self-determination and subordiation: The past, present and future of Native American governance. In *The State of Native America,* ed. A. Jaimes, pp. 87–122. Boston, Mass.: South End Press.

Rorty, R. 1992. Cosmopolitanism without emancipation: A response to Lyotard. In *Modernity and identity,* ed. S. Lash and J. Friedman, pp. 58–72. Cambridge: Blackwell.

Rogers, C. R. 1942. *Counseling and psychotherapy.* Boston: Houghton Mifflin.

———. 1961. *On becoming a person.* Boston: Houghton Mifflin.

Room, R. 1981) Alcohol, science and social control. In. *Alcohol, science and society revisited,* ed. E. Gomberg and W. Raskin, pp. 371–84. New Brenswick, N.J.: Rutgers Center of Alcohol Studies.

———. 1984. Alcohol control and public health. *Annual Review of Public Health,* 293–317.

Rush, B. 1948. *The autobiography of Benjamin Rush,* ed. George Corner. Princeton, N.J.: Princeton University Press.

Ryan, R. A., and J. D. Spence. 1978. American Native American mental health research: Local control and cultural sensitivity. *White Cloud Journal* 1: 15–18.

Said, E. 1978. *Orientalism.* New York: Pantheon

———. 1993. *Culture and imperialism.* New York: Alfred Knopf.

Sandner, D. F. 1972. Healing symbolism in Navajo religion. *Spring: An Annual of Archetypal Psychology and Jungian Thought*, 132–43.

———. 1979. *Navaho symbols of healing.* New York: Harvest/HBJ.

Schinke, F., M. Bebel, M. Orlandi, and G. Botvin. 1988. Strategies for vulnerable pupils: School social work practices to prevent substance abuse. *Urban Education* 22 (4): 510–19.

Schinke, S. P., M. A. Orlandi, G. Botvin, and L. Gilchrist. 1988. Preventing substance abuse among American Native American aldolescents: A bicultural competence skills approach. *Journal of Counseling Psychology* 35 (1) 87–90.

Sejorne, L. 1957. *Pensamiento religion en el Mexico antiguo.* Mexico City: University of Mexico.

Shen, W. W. 1986. The Hopi Native American's morning hallucinations. *Journal of Nervous and Mental Disease* 174 (6): 365–67.

Shen, W. W., A. M. Sanchez, and T. Huang. 1984. Verbal participation in group therapy: A comparative study on New Mexico ethnic groups. *Hispanic Journal of Behavioral Sciences* 6 (3): 277–84.

Shore, J., J. Kinzie, J. L. Hampson, and M. E. Pattison. 1973. Psychiatric epidemiology of a Native American village. *Psychiatry* 36 (1): 70–81.

Shoshan, T. 1989. Mourning and longing from generation to generation. *American Journal of Psychotherapy* 43 (2): 193–207.

Sinha, D. 1984. Psycholgy in the context of third world development. *International Journal of Psychology*, 17–29.

Slagle, L., and J. Weibel-Orlando. 1986. The Native American Shaker Church and Alcoholics Anonymous: Revitalistic curing cult. *Human Organization* 45 (4): 310–19.

Snake, R. 1976. Report on alcohol and drug abuse: Final report to the American Native American Policy Review Commission. Washington, D.C.: United States Government Printing Office.

Solomon, Z., M. Kotler, and M. Mikulincer. 1988. Combat-related post-traumatic stress disorder among second-generation Holocaust survivors: Preliminary findings. *American Journal of Psychiatry* 145 (7): 865–68.

Spaulding, J. M. 1986. Recent suicide rates among ten Ojibwa Native American bands in northwestern Ontario. *Omega: Journal of Death and Dying* 16 (4): 347–54.

Spiegelberg, H. 1972. *Phenomenology in psycholgy and psychiatry.* Evanston, Ill.: Northwestern University Press.

Spivak, G. 1988. Can the subaltern speak. In *Marxism and the interpretation of culture*, ed. C. Grossberg and N. L. Grossberg, pp. 271–313. Urbana: University of Illinois Press.

Stewart, O. C. 1977. Contemporary document on Wovoka prophet of the Ghost Dance. *Ethnohistory* 23 (3): 222.

Sue, S., and N. Zane. 1987. The role of culture and cultural techings in psychotherapy: A critique and reformation. *American Psychologist* 42: 37–45.

Snyder, P., ed. 1962. Cultural differences in the meaning of alcoholism. In *Society, culture and alcoholism.* Carbondale: Southern Illinois University Press.

Taussig, M. 1992. *The Nervous System.* New York: Routledge.

Thin Elk, G. 1990. *Red road series.* Vermillion: Medicine Wheel Inc.

Thomas, A., and S. Sillen. 1972. *Racism and Psychiatry.* New York: Brunnerland.

Thornton, R. 1986. *We shall live again: The 1870 and 1890 Ghost Dance movements as demographic revitalization.* ASA Rose Monograph Series: University of Minnesota.

Trimble, J. 1984. Drug abuse prevention research needs among American Native Americans and Alaskan natives. *White Cloud Journal* 3 (3): 22–34.

Trimble, J., A. Padilla, and C. Bell. 1987. Drug abuse among ethnic minorities. DHHS Pub (ADM) 87–1474, ed. Washington, D.C.: NIDA Office of Science Monograph.

Use of "detailed dolls" questioned. 1988. *APA Monitor*, June, p. 24.

Villanueva, M. 1989. Literature review. In *Suicide handbook: Prevention and intervention with Native Americans*, ed. E. Duran, pp. 13–36. Sacramento: IHS.

Wallace, A. F. 1969. *The death and rebirth of the Seneca.* New York: Vintage Books.

Wallerstein, N., and E. Bernstein . 1988. Empowerment education: Freire's ideas adapted to health education. *Health Education Quarterly* 15 (4): 379–94.

Weeks, P. 1990. Postcolonial challenges to grand theory. *Human Organization* 49 (3): 239.

Weibel-Orlando, J., T. Weisner, and K. A. Long. 1984. Urban and rural Native American drinking patterns: Implications for intervention. *Substance and Alcohol Actions/Misuse* 5 (1): 45–57.

Weisner, T., J. Weibel-Orlando, and K. A. Long. 1984. "Serious drinking," "white man's drinking," and "teetotalling": Drinking styles in an urban American Native American population. *Journal of Studies on Alcohol* 45 (3): 237–50.

Westermeyer, J., and J. Neider. 1984a. Depressive symptoms among Native American alcoholics at the time of a 10-year followup. *Alcoholism: Clinical and Experimental Research* 8 (5): 429–34.

Westermeyer, J., and J. Neider. 1984b. Predicting treatment outcomes after ten years among American Native American alcoholics. 8 (2): 179–84.

Westermeyer, J., and E. Peake. 1983. A ten-year follow-up of alcoholic Native Americans in Minnesota. *American Journal of Psychiatry* 140 (2): 189–94.

Williams, C. L., and J. W. Berry. 1991. Primary prevention of acculturative stress among refugees: Application of psychological theory and practice. *American Psychologist* 46 (6): 632–41.

Wilson, L. G., and J. H. Shore. 1975. Evaluation of a regional Native American alcohol program. *American Journal of Psychiatry* 132 (3): 225–58.

Winkler, A. M. 1968. Drinking on the American Indian frontier. *Quarterly Journal of Studies on Alcohol* 29 (June): 413–45.

Yellowthunder, L. 1981. Some thoughts on American Native American and Alaskan native chemical use. *White Cloud Journal* 2 (3): 35–36.

Index

Abbas, L., 29
acculturation, 32
Act, 159
Adams-Tucker, C., 160
Albino, 160
Alchemy, 67
alcohol spirits, 139,145
Alcoholics Anonymous, 102, 103
alcoholism rates, 24
Alkali Lake, 105
anesthesia, 37, 173
anesthesize, 143
anima, 81
animus, 81
anomie, 112
anthropologists, 25
anxiety, 24
Apache, 48
Archetypal psychology, 10
Arlee, J., 139
Asklepius, 47
assimilation, 8, 34
Assiniboin, 132
Atkins, E., 123
Augustinian, 80

Auld, 94, 145, 146
axis mundi, 78
Aztec, 66

Bach, P., 100
Barter, E., 96
Baynes, K., 113
Beauvais, F., 95
Bebel, M., 114
Bell, R., 113
Benedekt, E., 160
bereavement, 32
Berkhoffer, R., 107, 117, 118, 119
Berlin, I., 95, 96
Bernardino de Sahagun, 67
Bernstein, E., 199
Berry, 32
binary opposites, 5
biological determinism, 18
black world, 36, 38, 40
Black Elk, 4, 68
blaming the victim, 28
Blauner, R., 198
Blum, K., 98
boarding schools, 27, 28, 33

Bogue, R., 35, 110
Bornstein, P., 100
Borunda, Z., 96
Bowman, A., 113
Bowyer, A., 161
Bozlee, S., 99
Buddhist, 70

Campbell, J., 48, 75
Canguilhem, G., 107
canonical texts, 25
Canvas Dancing, 138
Caplan, G., 187, 197
Carafides, J., 194
Carmichael, S., 185
Carpenter, R., 100
Cartesian, 113
Cartesian anxiety disorder, 7
Cartier, 122
catharsis, 30, 158
catharting anger, 29
centered therapist, 65
Cheek, D., 163
chemical dependency, 158
chemical abuse, 160
Children's Apperception Test, 166, 169
Chippewa, 123, 132
CHR, 178
Christ, 134, 145
Christian, 181, 197
cirrhosis, 106
Clark, D., 163
Claude Levi-Straus, 57
Clements, F., 19
clinical relevance, 19
Colins, S., 118
collective anesthesia, 65
colonial mind set, 6
colonial discourse, 109, 116, 127
Colonial ideology, 120
colonialistic paradigm, 87
Comanche, 133, 134
community cohesion, 41
compartmentalize, 90, 140

conquest, 24
Conrad, R., 95
conscientizacao, 126
Corn Planter, 129
cosmological paradigm, 86
counterhegemonic, 27, 119, 126, 136
creation, 15
Cree, 130, 132
cross cultural, 162, 165
cross-cultural 4, 9, 17, 56, 59, 87, 115
cross-tribal, 49
cult, 43
cultural revitalization, 128
cultural reproduction, 28
cultural hegemony, 104
Curry, A., 38
Custer, 152

death rebirth, 63
DeBlassie, R., 95
Delaware, 134
Deloria, 15, 107, 115, 176
depression, 24
Derrida, 116
Derridian, 26
Descartes, 47, 74
diseased object, 20
dishonored treaties, 24
Draw-a-Person, 166
dropouts, 24
DSM-IV, 52
Dunham, Captain, 132
Duran, E., 29, 87, 88, 102, 196

Earth spirits, 82
Economic competition, 33
Edgerton, R., 103, 119, 122
Edmunds, 132
Edshu, 75
Edwards, 95, 97, 99, 113, 114
ego strength, 165
ego inflation, 60
emotional arousal, 60

environmental shock, 32
epistemic violence, 25, 52
epistemological forms, 5, 10
Eskimo, 48
ethnic strata, 66, 66
ethnocide, 27, 28, 53, 101, 159
ethnographic, 50, 61
ethnologist, 46
eugenics, 5
Eurocentric, 25, 110, 125, 135, 136
European mind-set, 6
existential death, 39
exploitation, 15
extermination, 27, 33
extroversion, 70, 71, 72, 74

family system, 31
Fannon, F., 4, 6, 14, 186
Fejervay, Father, 66
feminine cosmology, 72
feminist studies, 5
Fermin, Father, 46
fetal alcohol syndrome, 99
Fingarette, 112
first contact, 32
fisher, 95
Foucault, M., 7, 26, 113
Foulks, E., 97
fourth worlds, 6
Fox, R., 108
Franklin, Benjamin, 125
Freidman, 113
Freire, P., 126, 158, 198
French & Hornbuckle, 29
Freud, S., 50, 59
Freudian, 17
Fuqua, D., 97
Futterman, S., 98

Gayton, A., 49, 61
Gazay, L., 96
generationally cumulative, 31
genocide, 6, 27, 28, 87, 101, 152, 174

Ghost Dance, 134
Gifford, E., 49
Graves, T., 96
Great League, 129
Guha, R., 26, 113
Guillory, B., 105

Habermas, 116
Handelman, 48
Handsome Lake, 48, 109, 126, 127, 128, 129, 130, 131, 132, 133, 135
Harmon, 108
harmony, 15, 16, 75, 179
Havighurst, R., 95
healer archetype, 61
hegemonic discourse, 110
hegemonic social science, 109
hegemonic, 52
hegemony, 6, 7, 69, 87, 88, 90
heirosgamos, 70
Hersch, J., 59
Hertzberg, 133, 134
Hiawatha, 68
Hillman, J., 64
Hippocratic tradition, 47
histographic, 25
Hodgkenson, H., 107
Hoffman, 96, 99
Holtzman, 99
Honigfeld, L., 100
Hudson, 122
Huehueteotl, 142
Huitzilopochtli, 66, 67
Hulme, J., 118
Hurlburt, 97
Hurons, 47
Husserl, 193
hybrid, 7
hybrid family systems, 34

identification with aggressor, 36
identity loss, 36
incest, 149, 150
indeginization, 126

Indian Tom, 120, 121
Indian Health Service (IHS), 94, 95, 98, 100, 106, 108, 147, 177, 189
Indian Reorganization Act, 137
indigenous, 15
Indigenous alcohol discourse, 125
inferior function, 72, 75, 81
initiation, 42, 43
institutional racism, 18
intelligence testing, 5
intergenerational, 154, 158
Intergenerational Posttraumatic Stress disorder, 30, 43
internalized oppression, 27, 28, 29
introversion, 70, 71, 74
intuition, 76, 78
Invasion War Period, 33
Iroquoise Confederacy, 127, 128
Iroquois, 47
Iyjugarjuk, 48

Jackson, 96, 99
Jacobs, 123
JanMohamed, 117
Jellinek, 111, 112
Jesuits, 46, 123
Jewish Holocaust, 31
Jilek-Aall, 95
Johnson, William, 124
Jung, 16, 17, 18, 19, 48 50, 59, 60, 63, 65, 66, 67, 68, 69, 70, 7172, 73, 74, 75, 76, 77, 78, 79, 80, 141, 145, 148, 194

Kahn, M., 95
Kalahari, 23
Kalff, D., 161
Kaplan, D., 100
Katz, P., 96, 97
Kennedy, J., 186
Kickapoo, 132
Kiowa, 133
Kivalahan, D., 97
Kline, J. 97

Kotter, M., 31
Krell, R., 31
Kulka, R., 172
Kurtz, E., 102

LaBoueff, S., 95
lactification, 4
LaFramboise, T., 87
Lalawethika, 130
Lash, 113
Lefley, H., 87, 101
Leland, J., 111, 112
Lemert, E., 124
Letakots-Lesa, 55
libido, 80
lifeworld, 9, 28, 42, 87, 89, 110
linguistic turn, 5
literary criticism, 5
Lockhart, B., 153
logical positivism, 7, 45
Long, K., 95, 123
Long House Religion, 109
loss and separation, 32
Lowenfeld, M., 161
Lurie, N., 115

MacAndrew, C., 103, 119, 122
Macdonell, D., 117
Mann, 112
masculine cosmology, 82
Mason, P., 117
matriarchal, 81
May, P., 95, 105, 113
Mayan, 66
McCarthy, T., 113
McShane, 99
medicine bundles, 132
medicine, 37, 39, 41, 59, 77, 88, 89, 98, 140, 148
Mescalero Apache, 133
Mesoamerican, 141, 142
methodological, 25, 26
Mexico, 67, 133
Mikulincer, M., 31
MMPI, 97

Mohawk, 128
Mohican, 132
Mondamin, 68
Moody, B., 59, 62
Morgan, P., 103
Mosher, J., 103, 104, 124
Mountain Lake, 80
Murphy, S., 95
Murray, D., 25
myth, 24, 45, 65, 95
Myths, 141

N. Scott Momaday, 107
Naskapi, 115, 116
Native American Church, 98, 109, 126, 133, 134
Native Shaker Church, 135
Native Social Movements, 107
Native American Self Determination and Education Assistance Act, 24
Navaho Medicine Man, 58
Navaho, 75
Nazi Holocaust, 30
neglect, 24
Neider, J., 96, 98
neocolonialism, 5
Nietzsche, 73, 148
NIMH, 176
noble savage, 44, 115, 118
noncompartmentalization, 15
Northfork Mono, 49

Ochberg, F., 172
Odin, 66
Oetting, E., 95, 99
old world motifs, 66
oppositional identity, 118
Orlandi, 100, 114
orthodox, 19, 21, 45, 88, 94, 106, 164
Ottawas, 132

Padilla, A., 113, 114
pahtology, 112

Palenque, 66
pan Indian, 109
pan-native, 127, 129
Papago, 121
participation mystique, 44, 69, 75
Pascarosa, 98
paternalistic, 104
pathological, 97, 99, 165
patriarchal worldview, 81
Pedersen, P., 87
Pelz, M., 96
Perry, J., 64
personality, 97
Peterson, K., 40
Peyote, 98, 134, 136
Phenomenological, 166
phenomenology, 193
philosophical imperialism, 25
phrenes, 79
Plato, 17
politically discursive, 27
positivism, 6
postcolonial paradigm, 6
postcolonial, 106, 109, 126, 136
postmodern, 116
Potowatami, 132
precolonization lifeworld, 37
Prognostic expectation, 59
Prout, M., 40
psychometric, 18
psychopathology, 96, 101
PTSD paradigm, 40
purification, 47

Quakers, 128
Quanah Parker, 134
Query, 97, 99
Quetzalcoatl, 142

racism, 95
racist, 18
Ragueneau, 47
Raymond, M., 94, 137, 138, 139, 140, 144, 154
recidivism, 106

refugee syndrome, 33, 34
Resnick, H., 95
revitalization, 105, 127, 133
Rhoades, E., 108
Robbins, R., 115
Rogers, 56, 62
Room, R., 103, 112
root metaphors, 18
Rorty, R., 26
Rowe, W., 87
Rush, B., 120, 121
Ryan, R., 176

Said, E., 116
Samuels, B., 96
Sanchez, A., 97
Sandner, D., 56, 57, 58
sandtray, 10, 161, 162, 164, 165, 169, 170
satanic, 43
Schinke, F., 100, 114
Schwarz, 40
scientific discourse, 5, 27
Scientism, 78
Sejourne, L., 141, 142
Self Determination, 198
self-hatred, 28, 29
Seneca, 128, 129, 132
sensation, 76, 78
Seventh Sacred Direction, 76, 77, 140, 142
sexual abuse, 34
Shawnee, 130, 131, 132, 133
Shawnee prophet, 135
Shen,W., 96, 97
Shetky, D., 160
Shore, J., 95, 96, 98
Shoshan, T., 30
Shuswap, 105
Sinha, D., 25, 26
Sitting Bull, 19
Six Nations, 129
Slagle, L., 125, 135
smudging, 148, 182
Snake, R., 191

sociohistorical, 27, 95, 101, 162
Socrates, 47
Solomon, Z., 31
sorcery, 21
soul wound, 194
soul loss, 20
soul wound, 24, 45
Spaulding, J., 95
Spence, J., 176
Spiegelberg, H., 193, 194
spirit of alcohol, 93
spirit intrusion, 20
Spirit intrusion, 144
Spivak, G., 25, 113
Stanley Sue, 8
Stephen Gould, 18
Stewart, 134
subject-object, 47
subjectivity, 7
subjugate, 27
subjugation, 33, 104, 107
Subjugation and Reservation Period, 33
Sue, S., 83
sweat lodge, 89, 183
symbols, 16

taboo, 20, 21
Taussig, M., 116
Teasdale, J., 163
technologies of power, 26
Tecumseh, 109, 131, 132
Templo Mayor de Tenochitlan, 142
Tenskatawa, 135
Tenskwatawa, 109, 126, 130, 131, 132, 133
Teotihuacan, 142
termination, 28, 34
Tezcatlipoca, 67
Thematic Apperception Test, 162, 165, 168
therapist centered, 74, 77, 85
Thin Elk, G., 76, 77
Thornton, R., 27, 30
Tippecanoe, 133, 135

Tlaloc, 141, 142
Toxcatl ,67
tradition, 146, 147, 148, 149, 151,
   155
tradition, 9, 16, 19, 21, 35, 37, 39,
   41, 44, 52, 57, 77, 87, 88, 89,
   90, 94, 105, 106, 140
traditional healers, 172, 180
traditional, 135
traditional, 174
traditional homelands, 33
traditional cosmology, 86, 90
traditional healing, 90
traditional family, 34
traditional healers, 50
traditional lifeworld, 38
traditional economies, 105
traditional symbolism, 58
traditional economy, 35
Trail of Tears, 153
transcendent, 78
transcendent function, 16
transhistorical, 26
trauma mastery, 42, 86
Treaty of Paris, 127
Treaty of Fort Stanwix, 128
tribal lifeworld, 35
Trimble, J., 113, 114
Tsonnontouens (Seneca), 46
typological paradigm, 76
typological constructs, 70
typology, 71, 74, 75, 82

universal subject, 5
unresolved trauma, 44
unresolved grief, 42
utilitarian worldview, 26
utilitarian, 33
utilization rates, 8

Vietnam era PTSD, 172
Villanueva, M., 177

Wakan Tanka, 76
Wallace, A., 46, 47, 48, 129, 130,
   131
Wallerstein, 199
warrior tradition, 39, 43
warrior archetype, 38
Washo, 48
Weeks, P., 125
Weibel-Orlando, 96, 125, 135
Weisner, T., 96
Westermeyer, J., 96, 98
western subjectivity, 5
Western worldview, 78
white superiority, 19
Wild Man, 117
Williams, 114
Williams, C. L., 32
Williams, Roger, 119
Willie, 105
Wilson, 98
Wilson, John, 134
Wilson Jack, 134
Winkler, 123
worldview, 197
worldview, 10, 15, 17, 25, 34, 46,
   51, 64, 75, 80, 85, 98
Wovoka, 134
Wukchumni, 62
Wyandot, 132

Yellowthunder, L., 96

Zane, N., 83
Zarathustra, 77
Zuni, 121